THE
WASHINGTON
BALTIMORE
MOUNTAIN
BIKE
BOOK

THE WASHINGTON BALTIMORE *MOUNTAIN BIKE* BOOK

OUT OF THE GRIDLOCK
INTO THE WOODS

by Scott Adams

Beachway Press

Maps by Scott Adams
Cover illustration by Todd Sprow
Illustrations by Todd Sprow, Mike Francis, and Walt Wait
Cover design by Theron Moore
Photos by Scott Adams (unless noted otherwise)
Editing by John Phillips
ISBN 1-882997-03-4

Library of Congress Cataloging-in-Publication Data
Adams, Scott
The Washington-Baltimore Mountain Bike Book
Out of the Gridlock — Into the Woods
First Edition
94-070940
CIP

Published by Beachway Press
9201 Beachway Lane
Springfield, VA 22153

Printed in the United States of America

10 9 8 7 6 5 4 3

Table of Contents

To my parents.

Introduction

Welcome to the new generation of bicycling!

Indeed, the sport has changed tremendously from the sleek geometry and lightweight frames of the racing bicycle. While still the heart and soul of bicycling worldwide, road bikes have lost ground in recent years, *unpaving* the way for the mountain bike, which is now accountable for the majority of all bicycle sales in the U.S. With this change comes a new breed of cyclist, less concerned with smooth roads and long rides, who thrives in places once inaccessible to the mortal road bike.

The mountain bike, with its knobby tread and reinforced frame, takes cyclists to places once unheard of on a bike — down rugged mountain trails, through streams of rushing water and thick mud, across the frozen Alaskan tundra, and even to work in the city. There seem to be few limits on what this fat-tired beast can do and where it can take us. Few obstacles stand in its way, few boundaries slow its progress. Nothing, it seems, can stop the mountain bike from becoming the pre-eminent bicycle in the world — nothing that is, except its own success.

If trail closure means little to you now, read on and discover how a trail can be here today and gone tomorrow. With so many new off-road cyclists each year taking to the trails, it's no wonder trail access hinges precariously between universal acceptance and complete termination. But a little work on your part can go a long way in preserving trail access for use in the future. Nothing is more crucial to the survival of mountain biking itself than to read the following pages and practice their examples. Then turn to the maps, pick your favorite rides, and hit the dirt!

WHAT THIS BOOK IS ABOUT

Within these pages you will find everything you need to know about off-road bicycling in the Washington-Baltimore area. It begins by exploring the fascinating history of the mountain bike itself, then goes on to discuss everything from the health benefits of off-road cycling to tips and techniques for bicycling over logs and up hills. Also included are the types of clothing to keep you comfortable and in style, essential equipment ideas to keep your rides smooth and trouble-free, and descriptions of off-road terrain to prepare you for the kinds of bumps and bounces you can expect to encounter. Perhaps the two major thrusts of this book, though, are its unique and detailed maps and its relentless dedication to trail preservation.

Each of the 25 rides included in this book is accompanied by four very different maps. A location map shows you where each ride is in relation to the rest of the Washington-Baltimore area, a 3D surface area map gives you a fascinating view of the surrounding topography and landscape, the road map leads you through each ride and is accompanied by detailed directions, and the 3D profile map shows you in three dimensions an accurate view of the each ride's ups and downs.

Without open trails, the maps in this book are virtually useless. Cyclists must learn to be responsible for the trails they use and to share these trails with others. This book addresses such issues as why trail use has become so controversial, what can be done to improve our image, how to have fun *and* ride responsibly, on-the-spot trail repair techniques, trail maintenance hotlines for each trail in the book, and the worldwide-standard *Rules of the Trail*.

All 25 rides are complete with maps, trail descriptions and directions, local anecdotes and history, and a quick-reference information board with useful trail-maintenance hotline numbers.

It's important to note, when discussing off-road cycling, that mountain bike rides tend to take longer than road rides because the average speed is often much slower. Average speeds can vary from a climbing pace of three to four miles per hour to 12 to 13 miles per hour on flatter roads and trails. Keep this in mind when planning your trip.

MOUNTAIN BIKE BEGINNINGS

It seems the mountain bike, originally designed for lunatic adventurists bored with straight lines, clean clothes, and smooth tires, has become globally popular in as short a time as it would take to race down a mountain trail.

Like most things of a revolutionary nature, the mountain bike was born on the west coast. But unlike roller blades, purple hair, and the peace sign, the concept of the off-road bike cannot be credited solely to the imaginative Californians. They were just the first to make waves.

The design of the first off-road specific bike was based on the geometry of the old Schwinn Excelsior, a one-speed, camel-back cruiser with balloon tires. Joe Breeze was the creator behind them, and in 1977 he built 10 of these "Breezers" for himself and his friends from Marin County, California, at $750 apiece — a bargain.

Breeze was a serious competitor in bicycle racing, placing 13th in the 1977 U.S. Road Racing National Championships. After races, he and his friends would scour local bike shops hoping to find old bikes they could then restore.

It was the 1941 Schwinn Excelsior for which Breeze paid just five dollars that began to shape and change bicycling history forever. After taking the bike home, removing the fenders, oiling the chain, and pumping up the tires, Breeze hit the dirt. He loved it.

His inspiration, while forerunning, was not altogether unique. On the opposite end of the country, nearly 2,500 miles from Marin County, east coast bike bums were also growing restless. More and more old, beat-up clunkers were being restored and modified. These behemoths often weighed as much as 80 pounds and were so reinforced they seemed virtually indestructible. But rides that take just 40 minutes on today's 25-pound featherweights took the steel-toed-boot- and blue-jean-clad bikers of the late 1970s and early 1980s nearly four hours to complete.

It wasn't until 1981 that it was possible to purchase a production mountain bike, but local retailers found these ungainly bicycles difficult to sell and rarely kept them in stock. By 1983, however, mountain bikes were no longer such a fringe item, and large bike manufacturers quickly jumped into the action, producing their own versions of the off-road bike. By the 1990s, the mountain bike had firmly established its place with bicyclists of nearly all ages and abilities and now commands nearly 90% of the U.S. bike market.

There are many reasons for the mountain bike's success in becoming the hottest two-wheeled vehicle in the nation. They are much friendlier to the cyclist than traditional road bikes because of their comfortable upright position and shock-absorbing fat tires. And because of the health-conscious, environmentalist generation of the late 1980s and 1990s, people are more activity minded and seek nature on a closer front than paved roads can allow. The mountain bike gives you these things and takes you far away from the daily grind — even if you're only minutes from the Beltway.

MOUNTAIN BIKING INTO SHAPE

If your objective is to get in shape and lose weight, then you're on the right track, because mountain biking is one of the best ways to get started.

One way many of us have lost weight in this sport is the crash-and-burn-it-off method. Picture this — You're speeding uncontrollably down a vertical drop that you realized you shouldn't be on only after it was too late. Your front wheel lodges into a rut the size of Grand Canyon and launches you through endless weeds, trees, and pointy rocks before coming to an abrupt halt in a puddle of thick mud. Surveying the damage, you discover, with the layers of skin, body parts, and lost confidence littering the trail above, that those unwanted pounds have been shed — permanently.

There is, of course, a more conventional *(and quite a bit less painful)* approach to losing weight and gaining fitness on a mountain bike. It's called the workout, and bicycles provide an ideal way to get physical. Take a look at some of the benefits associated with cycling.

Cycling helps you shed pounds without gimmicky diet fads or weight-loss programs. You can explore the countryside and burn nearly 10 to 16 calories per minute or close to 600 to 1000 calories per hour. Moreover, it's a great way to spend an afternoon.

No less significant than the external and cosmetic changes of your body from riding are the internal changes taking place. Over time, cycling regularly will strengthen your heart as your body grows vast networks of new capillaries to carry blood to all those working muscles. This will, in turn, give your skin a healthier glow. The capacity of your lungs may increase up to 20%, and your resting heart rate will drop significantly. The Stanford University School of Medicine reports to the American Heart Association that people can reduce their risk of heart attack by nearly 64% if they can burn up to 2000 calories per week. This is only two to three hours of bike riding!

Recommended for insomnia, hypertension, indigestion, anxiety, and even for recuperation from major heart attacks, bicycling can be an excellent cure-all as well as a great preventive. Cycling just a few hours a week can improve your figure and sleeping habits, give you greater resistance to illness, increase your energy levels, and give you a feeling of accomplishment and heightened self-esteem.

BE SAFE — KNOW THE LAW

Occasionally, even the hard-core off-road cyclists will find they have no choice but to ride the pavement. When you are forced to hit the road, it's important for you to know and understand the rules.

Outlined below are a few of the common laws found in Virginia, Maryland, and D.C.'s Vehicle Code books.

- **Bicycles are legally classified as vehicles in Virginia, Maryland, and Washington, D.C.** This means that as a bicyclist, you are responsible for obeying the same rules of the road as a driver of a motor vehicle.
- **Bicyclists must ride *with* the traffic — *NOT AGAINST IT!*** Because bicycles are considered vehicles, you must ride your bicycle just as you would drive a car — *with traffic*. Only pedestrians should travel against the flow of traffic.
- **You must obey all traffic signs.** This includes stop signs and stop lights.
- **Always signal your turns.** Most drivers aren't expecting bicyclists to be on *their* roads, and many drivers would prefer that cyclists stay off *their* roads altogether. It's important, therefore, to clearly signal your intentions to motorists both in front of and behind you.
- **Bicyclists are entitled to the same roads as cars *(except controlled-access highways)*.** Unfortunately, cyclists are rarely given this consideration.
- **Be a responsible cyclist.** Do not abuse your rights to ride on open roads. Follow the rules and set a good example for all of us as you roll along.

THE MOUNTAIN BIKE CONTROVERSY

Are Mountain Bikes Environmental Outlaws?
Do We have the Right to Use Public Trails?

We have long endured the animosity of people in the back-country who complain about the consequences of mountain biking. Many people believe that our fat tires and knobby tread do unacceptable environmental damage and our uncontrollable riding habits are a danger to animals and to other trail users. To the contrary, mountain bikes have no more environmental impact than hiking boots or horse shoes. This does not mean, however, that mountain bikes leave no imprint at all. Wherever man treads, there is an impact. By riding responsibly, though, it is possible to leave only a minimum impact, something we all must take care to achieve.

Unfortunately, it is often people of great influence who view the mountain bike as the environment's worst enemy. Consequently, we as mountain bike riders and environmentally concerned citizens must be educators, impressing upon everyone that we also deserve the right to use these trails. Our responsibilities as bicyclists are no more and no less than any other trail user. We must all take the soft-cycling approach and show that mountain bikes are not environmental outlaws.

ETIQUETTE OF MOUNTAIN BIKING

Moving softly across the land means leaving no more than an echo
                                                            Hank Barlow

When discussing mountain biking etiquette, we are in essence discussing the soft-cycling approach. This term, as mentioned before, describes the art of minimum-impact bicycling and should apply to both the physical and social dimensions of the sport. But make no mistake — it is possible to ride fast and furiously while still maintaining the balance of soft-cycling. Here first are a few ways to minimize the *physical* impact of mountain bike riding.

- **Stay on the trail.** Don't ride around fallen trees or mud holes that block your path. Stop and cross over them. When you come to a vista overlooking a deep valley, don't ride off the trail for a better vantage point. Instead, leave the bike and walk to see the view. Riding off the trail may seem inconsequential when done just once, but soon someone else will follow, then others, and the cumulative results can be catastrophic. Each time you wander from the trail you begin creating a new path, adding one more scar to the earth's surface.
- **Do not disturb the soil.** Follow a line within the trail that will not disturb or damage the soil.
- **Do not ride over soft or wet trails.** After a rain shower or during the thawing season, trails will often resemble muddy, oozing swampland. The best thing to do is stay off the trails altogether. Realistically, however, we're all going to come across some muddy trails we cannot anticipate. Instead of blasting through each section of mud, which may seem both easier and more fun, lift the bike and walk past. Each time a cyclist rides through a soft or muddy section of trail, that part of the trail is permanently damaged. Regardless of the trail's conditions, however, remember always to go *over* the obstacles across the path, **NOT AROUND THEM.** Stay on the trail.

- **Avoid trails that, for all but God, are considered impassable and impossible.** Don't take a leap of faith down a kamikaze descent on which you will be forced to lock your brakes and skid to the bottom, ripping the ground apart as you go.

   Soft-cycling should apply to the *social dimensions* of the sport as well, since mountain bikers are not the only folks who use the trails. Hikers, equestrians, cross-country skiers, and other outdoors people use many of the same trails and can be easily spooked by a marauding mountain biker tearing through the trees. Be friendly in the forest and give ample warning of your approach.

- **Take out what you bring in.** Don't leave broken bike pieces and banana peels scattered along the trail.
- **Be aware of your surroundings.** Don't use popular hiking trails for race training.
- **Slow down!** Rocketing around blind corners is a sure way to ruin an unsuspecting hiker's day. Consider this — If you're flying down a quick singletrack descent at 20 mph, hit the brakes, and slow down to only six mph to pass someone, you're still moving twice as fast as they are!

   Like the trails we ride on, the social dimension of mountain biking is very fragile and must be cared for responsibly. By riding in the backcountry with caution, control, and responsibility, our presence should be felt positively by other trail users. Doing this, trail riding, a privilege that can quickly be taken away, will continue to be ours to share.

TRAIL MAINTENANCE

Unfortunately, despite all of the preventive measures we take to avoid trail damage, we're still going to run into a bunch of trails requiring our attention. This isn't to say we didn't ride responsibly or do our part to ease the burden on the earth. Simply put, a lot of people — hikers, equestrians, and cyclists alike, use the same trails. Some wear and tear is unavoidable. But, like your bike, if you want to use these trails for a long time to come, you must also maintain them.

Trail maintenance and restoration can be accomplished in a variety of ways. One way is for mountain bike clubs to combine efforts with other trail users (ie. hikers and equestrians) and work closely with land managers to cut new trails or repair existing ones. This not only reinforces to others the commitment cyclists have in caring for and maintaining the land, but also breaks the ice that often separates cyclists from their fellow trailmates. Another good way to help out is to show up on a Saturday morning with a few riding buddies at your favorite off-road domain ready to work. With a good attitude, thick gloves, and the local land manager's supervision, trail repair is fun and very rewarding. It's important, of course, that you arrange a trail-repair outing with the local land manager *before* you start pounding shovels into the dirt. They can lead you to the most needy sections of trail and instruct you on what repairs should be done and how best to accomplish the task. Perhaps the most effective means of trail maintenance, however, can be done by yourself and while you're riding. Read on.

On-The-Spot Quick Fix

Most of us, when we're riding, have at one time or another come upon muddy trails or fallen trees blocking our path. We notice that over time the mud gets deeper and the trail gets wider as people go through or around the obstacles. We worry that the problem will become so severe and repairs too difficult that the trail's access may be threatened. We also know that our ambition to do anything about it is greatest *at that moment*, not after a hot shower and plate of spaghetti. Here are a few on-the-spot quick fixes you can do that will hopefully correct a problem before it gets out of hand, and get you back on your bike within minutes.

- **Muddy Trails**. *What do you do when trails develop huge mud holes destined for the E.P.A.'s super-fund status?* The technique is called **corduroying**, and it works much like building a pontoon over the mud to support bikes, horses, or hikers as they cross. A corduroy *(not the pants)* is the term for roads made of logs laid down crosswise. Use small and medium-sized sticks and lay them side by side across the trail until they cover the length of the muddy section *(break the sticks to fit the width of the trail)*. Press them into the mud with your feet, then lay more on top if needed. Keep adding sticks until the trail is firm. Not only will you stay clean as you cross, but the sticks may soak up some of the water and help the puddle to dry. This quick fix may last as long as a month before needing to be redone. And as time goes on, with new layers added to the trail, the soil will grow stronger, thicker and more resistant to erosion. This whole process may take less than five minutes, and you can be on your way, knowing the trail behind you is in good repair.

- **Leaving the trail.** *What do you do to keep cyclists from cutting corners and leaving the designated trail?* The solution is much simpler than you may think. (No, don't hire an off-road police force). Notice where people are leaving the trail and throw a pile of thick branches or brush along the path, or place logs across the opening to block the way through. There are probably dozens of subtle tricks like these that will manipulate people to stay on the designated trail. If done well, no one will even notice that the thick branches scattered throughout the woods weren't always there. And most folks would probably rather take a moment to hop a log in the trail than get tangled in a mess of scratchy branches.

- **Obstacles in the way.** If there are large obstacles blocking the trail, try and remove them or push them aside. If you cannot do this by yourself, call the trail maintenance hotline to speak with the land manager of that particular trail and see what can be done.

We have to be willing to sweat *for* our trails in order to sweat *on* them. Police yourself and point out to others the significance of trail maintenance. "Sweat Equity," the rewards of continued land use won with a fair share of sweat, pays off when the trail is "up for review" by the land manager and he or she remembers the efforts made by trail-conscious mountain bikers.

RULES OF THE TRAIL

The International Mountain Bicycling Association (IMBA) has developed these guidelines to trail riding. These *Rules of the Trail* are accepted worldwide and will go a long way in keeping trails open. Please respect and follow these rules for everyone's sake.

1. **Ride on open trails only.** Respect trail and road closures (if you're not sure, ask a park or state official first), do not trespass on private property, and obtain permits or authorization if required. Federal and state wilderness areas are off-limits to cycling. Parks and state forests may also have certain trails closed to cycling.
2. **Leave no trace.** Be sensitive to the dirt beneath you. Even on open trails, you should not ride under conditions where you will leave evidence of your passing, such as on certain soils or shortly after a rainfall. Be sure to observe the different types of soils and trails you're riding on, practicing minimum-impact cycling. Never ride off the trail, don't skid your tires, and be sure to bring out at least as much as you bring in.
3. **Control your bicycle!** Inattention for even a second can cause disaster for yourself or for others. Excessive speed frightens and can injure people, gives mountain biking a bad name, results in trail closures, and has no excuses.
4. **Always yield.** Let others know you're coming well in advance (a friendly greeting is always good and often appreciated). Show your respect when passing others by slowing to walking speed or stopping altogether, especially in the presence of horses. Horses can be unpredictable, so be very careful. Anticipate that other trail users may be around corners or in blind spots.
5. **Never spook animals.** All animals are spooked by sudden movements, unannounced approaches, or loud noises. Give the animals extra room and time so they can adjust to you. Move slowly

or dismount around animals. Running cattle and disturbing wild animals are serious offenses. Leave gates as you find them, or as marked.

6. **Plan ahead.** Know your equipment, your ability, and the area in which you are riding, and plan your trip accordingly. Be self-sufficient at all times, keep your bike in good repair, and carry necessary supplies for changes in weather or other conditions. You can help keep trails open by setting an example of responsible, courteous, and controlled mountain bike riding.

7. **Always wear a helmet when you ride.** For your own safety and protection, a helmet should be worn whenever you are riding your bike. You never know when a tree root or small rock will throw you the wrong way and send you tumbling.

According to R.O.M.P., Responsible Organized Mountain Pedalers of Campbell, California, "thousands of miles of dirt trails have been closed to mountain bicycling because of the irresponsible riding habits of just a few riders." Don't follow the example of these offending riders. Don't take away trail privileges from thousands of others who work hard each year to keep the backcountry avenues open to us all.

THE NECESSITIES OF CYCLING

When discussing the most important things to have on a bike ride, cyclists generally agree on the following four items.

- **Helmet.** The reasons to wear a helmet should be obvious. Helmets are discussed in more detail in the *Be Safe — Wear Your Armor* section.
- **Water.** Without it, cyclists may face dehydration, resulting in dizziness and fatigue. On a warm day, cyclists should drink at least one full bottle during each hour of riding. Remember, it's always good to drink *before* you feel thirsty — otherwise, it may be too late.
- **Cycling Shorts.** These are necessary if you plan to ride your bike more than 20 to 30 minutes. Padded cycling shorts may be the only thing preventing your derriere from serious saddle soreness by ride's end. There are two types of cycling shorts you can buy. Touring shorts are good for people who don't want to look like they're wearing anatomically-correct cellophane. These look like regular athletic shorts with pockets, but have built-in padding in the crotch area for protection against chafing and saddle sores. The

more popular, traditional cycling shorts are made of skin-tight lycra material, also with a padded crotch. Whichever style you find most comfortable, cycling shorts are a necessity for long rides.

- **Food.** This essential item will keep you rolling. Cycling burns up a lot of calories and is among the few sports in which no one is safe from the "Bonk." Bonking feels like it sounds. Without food in your system, your blood sugar level collapses, and there is no longer any energy in your body. This instantly results in total fatigue and light-headedness. So when you're filling your water bottle, remember to bring along some food. Fruit, energy bars, or some other form of high-energy food are highly recommended. Candy bars are not, however, because they will deliver a sudden burst of high energy, then let you down soon after, causing you to feel worse than before. Energy bars are available at most bike stores and are similar to candy bars, but provide complex carbohydrate energy and high nutrition rather than the fast-burning simple sugars of candy bars.

BE PREPARED OR DIE

Essential equipment that will keep you from dying alone in the woods.

- **SPARE TUBE**
- **TIRE IRONS** — See the *Appendix* for instructions on fixing flat tires.
- **PATCH KIT**
- **PUMP**
- **MONEY** — Spare change to call home
- **SPOKE WRENCH**
- **SPARE SPOKES** — That fit your wheel. *Tape these to the chain stay.*
- **CHAIN TOOL**
- **ALLEN KEYS** — Bring appropriate sizes to fit your bike.
- **COMPASS**

- **FIRST AID KIT**
- **GUIDEBOOK** — In case all else fails and you must start a fire to survive, the guidebook will serve as an excellent fire starter.
- **MATCHES**

To carry these items, you may need a bike bag. A bag mounted in front of the handlebars provides quick access to your belongings, whereas a saddle bag fitted underneath the saddle keeps things out of your way. If you're carrying lots of equipment, you may want to consider a set of panniers. These are much larger and mount on either side of each wheel. Many cyclists, though, prefer not to use a bag at all. They just slip all they need into their jersey pockets, and off they go.

BE SAFE — WEAR YOUR ARMOR

While on the subject of jerseys, it's crucial we discuss the clothing you must wear to be safe, practical, and stylish. The following is a list of items that will save you from disaster, outfit you comfortably, and most important, keep you looking cool.

- **Helmet.** A helmet is an absolute necessity because it protects your head from complete annihilation. It is the only thing that will not disintegrate into a million pieces after a wicked crash on a descent you shouldn't have been on in the first place. A helmet with a solid exterior shell will also protect your head from sharp or protruding objects. Of course, with a hard-shelled helmet, you can also paste millions of stickers of your favorite bicycle manufacturers all over the outer shell, giving companies even more free advertising for your dollar.
- **Shorts.** Let's just say lycra cycling shorts are considered a major safety item if you plan to ride for more than 20 or 30 minutes at a time. As mentioned in *The Necessities of Cycling* section, cycling shorts are well regarded as the leading cure-all for chafing and saddle sores. The most preventive cycling shorts have padded "chamois" *(nowadays, most chamois is synthetic)* in the crotch area. Of course, if you choose to wear these traditional cycling shorts, it's imperative that they look as if someone spray painted them onto your body.

- **Gloves.** You may find well-padded cycling gloves invaluable when traveling over rocky trails and gravelly roads for hours on end. Long-fingered gloves may also be useful, as branches, trees, assorted hard objects, and, occasionally, small animals will reach out and whack your knuckles.
- **Glasses.** Not only do sunglasses give you an imposing presence *and* make you look cool *(both are extremely important)* they also protect your eyes from harmful ultraviolet rays, invisible branches, creepy bugs, dirt, and may prevent you from getting caught sneaking glances at a rider of the opposite sex who is also wearing skin-tight, revealing lycra.
- **Shoes.** Mountain bike shoes should have a stiff sole to help make pedaling easier, and should have good traction when walking your bike up a trail becomes necessary. Virtually any kind of good outdoor hiking footwear will work, but specific mountain bike shoes (especially those with inset cleats) are best. It is vital that these shoes look as ugly as humanly possible. Those closest in style to bowling shoes are, of course, the most popular.
- **Jersey or Shirt.** Bicycling jerseys are popular because of their snug fit and back pockets. When purchasing a jersey, look for ones that are loaded with bright, blinding, neon logos and manufacturers' names. These loudly decorated billboards are also good for drawing unnecessary attention to yourself just before taking a mean spill while trying to hop a curb. A cotton T-shirt is a good alternative in warm weather, but when the weather turns cold, cotton becomes a chilling substitute for the jersey. Cotton retains moisture and sweat against your body, which may cause you to get the chills and ills on those cold-weather rides.

OH, THOSE CHILLY CAPITAL CITY DAYS

If the weather chooses not to cooperate on the day you've set aside for a bike ride, it's helpful to be prepared.

- **Wear tights or leg warmers**. These are best in temperatures below 55 degrees. Knees are sensitive and can develop all kinds of problems if they get cold. Common problems include tendinitis, bursitis, and arthritis.

- **Wear plenty of layers on your upper body.** When the air has a nip in it, layers of clothing will keep the chill away from your chest and help prevent the development of bronchitis. If the air is cool, a polypropylene long-sleeved shirt is best. Be sure to wear this against the skin, beneath other layers of clothing. Polypropylene, like wool, wicks away moisture from your skin to keep your body dry. Try to avoid wearing cotton or baggy clothing when the temperature falls. Cotton, as mentioned before, holds moisture like a sponge, and baggy clothing catches cold air and swirls it around your body. Good cold-weather clothing should fit snugly against your body, but not be restrictive.
- **Wool socks for your feet.** Don't pack too many layers under those shoes, though. You might restrict the circulation, and your feet will get real cold, real fast.
- **Thinsulate or Gortex gloves.** We may all agree that there is nothing worse than frozen feet — unless your hands are frozen. A good pair of Thinsulate or Gortex gloves should keep your hands toasty and warm.

All of this clothing can be found at your local bike store, where the staff should be happy to help fit you into the seasons of the year.

TO HAVE OR NOT TO HAVE...
(Other Very Useful Items)

Though mountain biking is relatively new to the cycling scene, there is no shortage of things to buy for you and your bike to make riding better, safer, and easier. I have rummaged through the unending lists and separated the gadgets from the good stuff, coming up with what I believe are items certain to make mountain bike riding easier and more enjoyable.

- **Tires.** Buying yourself a good pair of knobby tires is the quickest way to enhance the off-road handling capabilities of your bike. There are many types of mountain bike tires on the market. Some are made exclusively for very rugged off-road terrain. These big-knobbed, soft rubber tires virtually stick to the ground with endless traction but tend to deteriorate quickly when ridden on pavement. There are other tires made exclusively for the road. These are called "slicks" and have no tread at all. For the average cyclist, though, a good tire somewhere in the middle of these two extremes should do the trick.

- **Toe Clips or Clipless Pedals.** With these, you will ride with more power. Toe clips attach to your pedals and strap your feet firmly in place, allowing you to exert pressure on the pedals on both the downstroke and the upstroke. They will increase your pedaling efficiency by 30% to 50%. Clipless pedals, which liberate your feet from the traditional straps and clips, have made toe clips virtually obsolete. Like ski bindings, they attach your shoe directly to the pedal. They are, however, much more expensive than toe clips.
- **Bar Ends.** These great clamp-on additions to your original straight bar will provide more leverage, an excellent grip for climbing, and a more natural position for your hands.
- **Fanny Pack.** These bags are ideal for carrying keys, extra food, guidebooks, tools, spare tubes, and a cellular phone, in case you need to call for help.
- **Suspension Forks.** For the more serious off-roaders who want nothing to impede their speed on the trails, investing in a pair of suspension forks is a good idea. Like tires, there are plenty of brands to choose from, and they all do the same thing — absorb the brutal beatings of a rough trail. The cost of these forks, however, is sometimes more brutal than the trail itself.
- **Bike Computers.** These are fun gadgets to own and are no longer quite as expensive to buy. They have such features as trip distance, speedometer, odometer, time of day, altitude, alarm, average speed, maximum speed, heart rate, global satellite positioning, etc., etc., etc. Bike computers will come in handy when following these maps or to show just how far you've ridden in the wrong direction.

TYPES OF OFF-ROAD TERRAIN

Before we begin roughing it off road, we may first have to ride the pavement to get where we're going. Please, don't be dismayed. Some of the best rides in the country are on the road. Once we get past these smooth-surfaced pathways, though, adventures in dirt await us.

- **Rails to Trails.** Abandoned rail lines are converted into useable public resources for exercising, commuting, or just enjoying nature. Old rails and ties are torn up and a trail, paved or unpaved, is laid along the existing corridor. This completes the cycle from ancient Indian trading routes, to railroad corridors, and back again to hiking and cycling trails.
- **Unpaved Roads.** These are typically found in rural areas and are

most often public roads. Be careful when exploring, though, not to ride on someone's unpaved private drive.

- **Fire Roads.** These dirt and gravel roads are used primarily as access to forest land and are kept in good condition. They are almost always open to public use.
- **Singletrack.** Singletrack can be the most fun on a mountain bike. These trails, with only one track to follow, are often narrow, challenging pathways through the woods. Remember to make sure these trails are open before zipping into the woods. *(At the time of this printing, all trails and roads in this guidebook were open to mountain bikes.)*
- **Open Land.** Unless there is a marked trail through a field or open space, you should not plan to ride here. Once one person cuts their wheels through a field or meadow, many more are sure to follow, causing irreparable damage to the landscape. A wise person once said, "Human tracks are like cancer cells, they spread very quickly."

TECHNIQUES TO SHARPEN YOUR SKILLS

Many of us see ourselves as pure athletes — blessed with power, strength, and endless endurance. However, it may be those with finesse, balance, agility, and grace that get around most quickly on a mountain bike. Although power, strength, and endurance do have their place in mountain biking, these elements don't necessarily form the framework for a champion mountain biker.

The bike should become an extension of your body. Slight shifts in your hips or knees can have remarkable results. Experienced bike handlers seem to flash down technical descents, dashing over obstacles in a smooth and graceful effort as if pirouetting in Swan Lake.

Here are some tips and techniques to help you connect with your bike and float gracefully over the dirt.

Braking

Using your brakes requires you to use your head, especially when descending. This doesn't mean using your head as a stopping block, but rather to think intelligently. Use your best judgment in terms of how much or how little to squeeze those brake levers.

The more weight a tire is carrying, the more braking power it has. When you're going downhill, your front wheel carries more weight than the rear. Braking with the front brake will help keep you in control without going into a skid. Be careful, though, not to overdo it with the front brakes and accidentally toss yourself over the handlebars. And don't neglect your rear brake! When descending, shift your weight back over the rear wheel, thus increasing your rear braking power as well. This will balance the power of both brakes and give you maximum control.

Good riders learn just how much of their weight to shift over each wheel and to apply just enough braking power to each brake, so as not to "endo" over the handlebars or skid down a trail.

Going Uphill
(Climbing Those Treacherous Hills)

- **Shift into a low gear** *(push the thumb shifter away from you)*. Before shifting, be sure to ease up on your pedaling so there is not too much pressure on the chain. Find the gear best for you that matches the terrain and steepness of each climb.
- **Stay seated.** Standing out of the saddle is often helpful when climbing steep hills with a road bike, but you may find that on dirt, standing may cause your rear tire to lose its grip and spin out. Climbing requires traction. Stay seated as long as you can, and keep the rear tire digging into the ground. Ascending skyward may prove to be much easier in the saddle.
- **Lean forward.** On very steep hills, the front end may feel unweighted and suddenly pop up. Slide forward on the saddle and lean over the handlebars. This will add more weight to the front wheel and should keep you grounded.
- **Keep pedaling.** On rocky climbs, be sure to keep the pressure on, and don't let up on those pedals! The slower you go through rough trail sections, the harder you will work.

Going Downhill
(The Real Reason We Get Up in the Morning)

- **Shift into the big chainring.** Shifting into the big ring before a bumpy descent will help keep the chain from bouncing off. And should you crash or disengage your leg from the pedal, the chain will cover the teeth of the big ring so they don't bite into your leg.

- **Relax.** Stay loose on the bike, and don't lock your elbows or clench your grip. Your elbows need to bend with the bumps and absorb the shock, while your hands should have a firm but controlled grip on the bars to keep things steady. Steer with your body, allowing your shoulders to guide you through each turn and around each obstacle.
- **Don't oversteer or lose control.** Mountain biking is much like downhill skiing, since you must shift your weight from side to side down narrow, bumpy descents. Your bike will have the tendency to track in the direction you look and follow the slight shifts and leans of your body. You should not think so much about steering, but rather in what direction you wish to go.
- **Rise above the saddle.** When racing down bumpy, technical descents, you should not be sitting on the saddle, but standing on the pedals, allowing your legs and knees to absorb the rocky trail instead of your rear.
- **Drop your saddle.** For steep, technical descents, you may want to drop your saddle three or four inches. This lowers your center of gravity, giving you much more room to bounce around.
- **Keep your pedals parallel to the ground.** The front pedal should be slightly higher so that it doesn't catch on small rocks or logs.
- **Stay focused.** Many descents require your utmost concentration and focus just to reach the bottom. You must notice every groove, every root, every rock, every hole, every bump. You, the bike, and the trail should all become one as you seek singletrack nirvana on your way down the mountain. But if your thoughts wander, then so may your bike, and into those trees you will go.

WATCH OUT!

Back-road Obstacles

- **Logs.** When you want to hop a log, throw your body back, yank up on the handlebars, and pedal forward in one swift motion. This clears the front end of the bike. Then quickly scoot forward and pedal the rear wheel up and over. Keep the forward momentum until you've cleared the log, and by all means, don't hit the brakes, or you may do some interesting acrobatic maneuvers!
- **Rocks.** Worse than Beltway potholes! Stay relaxed, let your elbows and knees absorb the shock, and always continue applying power to your pedals. Staying seated will keep the rear wheel weighted to prevent slipping, and a light front end will help you to respond quickly to each new obstacle. The slower you go, the more time your tires will have to get caught between the grooves.
- **Leaves.** Be careful of wet leaves. These may look pretty, but a trail covered with leaves may cause your wheels to slip out from under you. Leaves are not nearly as unpredictable and dangerous as ice, but they do warrant your attention on a rainy day.
- **Water.** Before crossing a stream or puddle, be sure to first check the depth and bottom surface. There may be an unseen hole or large rock hidden under the water that will have you all washed up if you're not careful. After you're sure all is safe, hit the water at a good speed, pedal steadily, and allow the bike to steer you through. Once you're across, tap the breaks to squeegee the water off the rims.

- **Mud.** If you must ride through mud, hit it head on and keep pedaling. You want to part the ooze with your front wheel and get across before it swallows you up. Above all, don't leave the trail to go around the mud. This just widens the path even more and leads to increased trail erosion.

Urban Obstacles

- **Curbs** are fun to jump, but as with logs, be careful.
- **Curbside Drains** are typically not a problem for bikes. Just be careful not to get a wheel caught in the grate.
- **Dogs** make great pets, but seem to have it in for bicyclists. If you think you can't outrun a dog that's chasing you, stop and walk your bike out of its territory. A loud yell to *Get!* or *Go home!* often works, as does a sharp squirt from your water bottle right between the eyes.
- **Cars** are tremendously convenient when we're in them, but dodging irate motorists in big automobiles becomes a real hazard when riding a bike. As a cyclist, you must realize most drivers aren't expecting you to be there and often wish you weren't. Stay alert and ride carefully, clearly signaling all of your intentions.
- **Potholes.** Like grates and back-road canyons, potholes should be avoided. Just because you're on an all-terrain bicycle doesn't mean you're indestructible. Potholes regularly damage rims, pop tires, and sometimes lift unsuspecting cyclists into a spectacular swan dive over the handlebars.

LAST-MINUTE CHECKOVER

Before a ride, it's a good idea to give your bike a once-over to make sure everything is in working order. Begin by checking the air pressure in your tires before each ride to make sure they are properly inflated. Mountain bikes require about 45 to 55 pounds per square inch of air pressure. If your tires are underinflated, there is greater likelihood that the tubes may get pinched on a bump or rock, causing the tire to flat.

Looking over your bike to make sure everything is secure and in its place is the next step. Go through the following checklist before each ride.

- **Pinch the tires to feel for proper inflation.** They should give just a little on the sides, but feel very hard on the treads. If you have a pressure gauge, use that.
- **Check your brakes.** Squeeze the rear brake and roll your bike forward. The rear tire should skid. Next, squeeze the front brake and roll your bike forward. The rear wheel should lift into the air. If this doesn't happen, then your brakes are too loose. Make sure the brake levers don't touch the handlebars when squeezed with full force.
- **Check all quick releases on your bike.** Make sure they are all securely tightened.
- **Lube up.** If your chain squeaks, apply some lubricant.
- **Check your nuts and bolts.** Check the handlebars, saddle, cranks, and pedals to make sure that each is tight and securely fastened to your bike.
- **Check your wheels.** Spin each wheel to see that they spin freely through the frame and between brake pads.
- **Have you got everything?** Make sure you have your spare tube, tire irons, patch kit, frame pump, tools, food, water, and guidebook.

Liability Disclaimer

Beachway Press assumes no liability for cyclists traveling along any of the suggested routes in this book. At the time of publication, all routes shown on the following maps were open to bicycles. They were chosen for their safety, aesthetics, and pleasure and are deemed acceptable and accommodating to bicyclists. Safety upon these routes, however, cannot be guaranteed. Cyclists must assume their own responsibility when riding these routes and understand that with an activity such as mountain bike riding, there may be unforeseen risks and dangers.

The Maps

I don't want anyone to feel restricted to just these roads and trails that I have mapped. Have an adventurous spirit and use these maps as a platform to dive into the Washington-Baltimore area's backcountry, discovering new and exciting routes for yourself. One of the best ways to begin is simply turn the map upside down and ride the course in reverse. The change in perspective is fantastic and the ride should feel wonderfully different.

For your own purposes, you may wish to copy the directions for the course you plan to ride onto a small sheet of paper, or perhaps photocopy the map and cue sheet to take with you. You could then fold these into a bike bag or stuff them into a jersey pocket. Just remember to slow down or even stop when you want to read the map.

MAP KEY

Interstate	⬠	Streams	〜〜〜
State Route	⬠	Power Lines	•—•—•—•
Primary Roadway	▬▬▬	Railroad Tracks	———
Paved Surface	———	County Borders	—--—--
Unpaved Surface	▬ ▬ ▬ ▬	Gates	⬤
Dirt Roads	=====	Directional Arrows	→
Trails	— — —	Start of Ride	★
Singletrack Route	-------	Easy	☺
Paved Route	▬▬▬▬	Moderate	■
Unpaved Route	=====	Difficult	◆

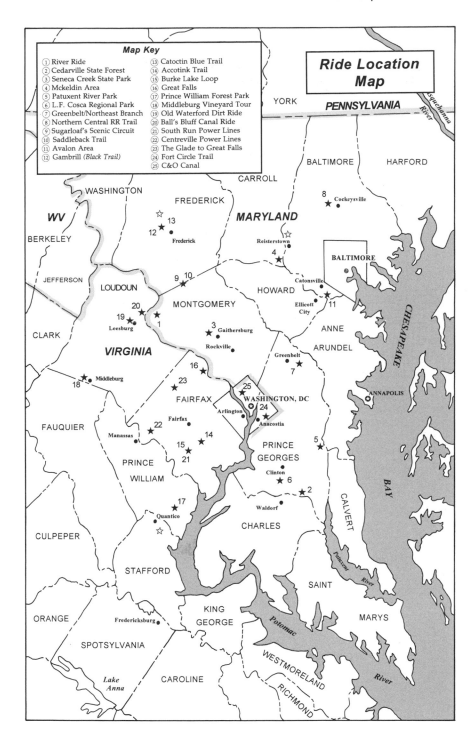

Map Key

1. River Ride
2. Cedarville State Forest
3. Seneca Creek State Park
4. Mckeldin Area
5. Patuxent River Park
6. L.F. Cosca Regional Park
7. Greenbelt/Northeast Branch
8. Northern Central RR Trail
9. Sugarloaf's Scenic Circuit
10. Saddleback Trail
11. Avalon Area
12. Gambrill (Black Trail)
13. Catoctin Blue Trail
14. Accotink Trail
15. Burke Lake Loop
16. Great Falls
17. Prince William Forest Park
18. Middleburg Vineyard Tour
19. Old Waterford Dirt Ride
20. Ball's Bluff Canal Ride
21. South Run Power Lines
22. Centreville Power Lines
23. The Glade to Great Falls
24. Fort Circle Trail
25. C&O Canal

Ride Location Map

Courses at a Glance

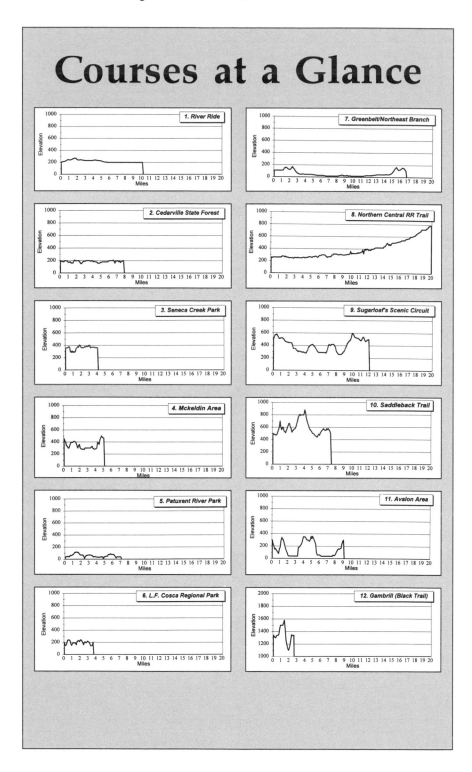

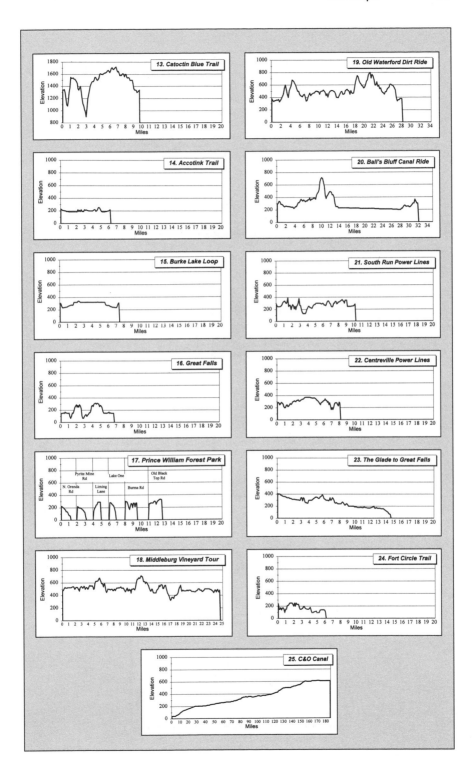

How To Use These Maps

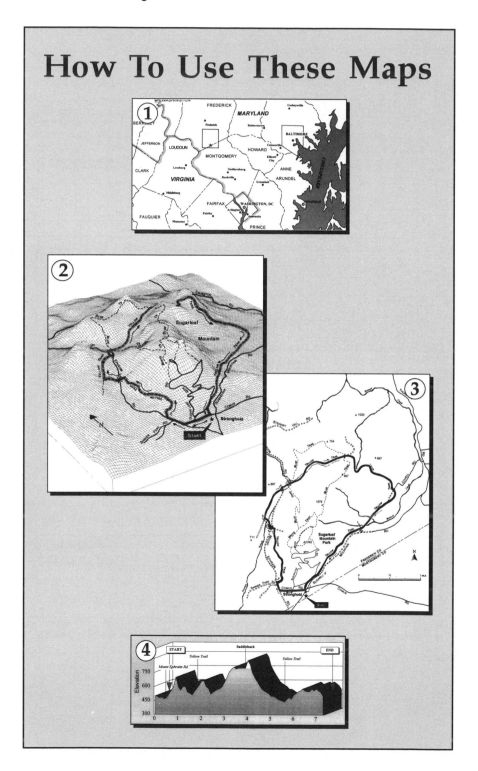

(1) **Location Map.** This map highlights the location and area covered by the two larger maps in that same section. This map should help conveniently pinpoint where the ride is in relation to the rest of the Washington-Baltimore area.

(2) **3D Surface Area Map.** This three-dimensional look at the earth's surface within the area of the selected ride gives you an accurate representation of the surrounding topography and landscape. The map has been rotated for the best view and includes most of the same features found on the road map.

(3) **Road Map.** This is your primary guide to each ride. It shows all of the accessible roads and trails, points of interest, water, towns, landmarks, and geographical features. It also distinguishes trails from roads and paved roads from unpaved roads. The selected route is highlighted, and directional arrows point the way.

(4) **3D Profile Map.** This three-dimensional profile gives you a cross-sectional look at the ride's ups and downs. Elevation is labeled on the left, mileage is indicated on the bottom, towns and points of interest are shown above the map in **bold**. Road and trail names, also shown above the map, are labeled in *italics*.

Ride Information Board (*At the end of each ride section*). This is a small bulletin board with important information concerning each ride.

- The **Trail Maintenance Hotline** is the direct number for the local land managers in charge of all the trails within the selected ride. Use this hotline right away if there is ever a problem with trail erosion, damage, or misuse.
- **Cost.** What money, if any, you may need to carry with you for park entrance fees or tolls.
- **Schedule.** This tells you at what times trails open and close, if on private or park land.
- **Maps.** This is a list of other maps to supplement the maps in this book. They are listed in order from most detailed to most general.

1. River Ride

Start: *Whites Ferry*	**Terrain:** *Hard dirt, unpaved roads*
Length: *10 miles*	**Riding Time:** *45 mins – 1 hour*
Rating: *Easy*	**Calories Burned:** *500 – 1000*

This easygoing loop along the Potomac River connects two points in time that signify an age when the ferry was the most convenient means across the river. The ride begins at Whites Ferry and travels south along flat dirt roads to Edwards Ferry, which quit operations in 1936.

At one point, during the 1700s, there were at least seven ferries serving the Loudoun area across the Potomac. Records of the county court show that by the end of the eighteenth century, not long after the signing of our Declaration of Independence, five ferries crossed the Potomac, connecting the Maryland and Virginia shores, one of which was Edwards. Whites Ferry, formerly known as Conrad's Ferry, began operations in 1836, carrying horse-drawn wagons, merchants, and supplies from shore to shore. Later in the nineteenth century, however, Whites and Edwards Ferries served quite different purposes.

During the Civil War, Union and Confederate troops used the ferries to carry troops back and forth across the Potomac both to advance and retreat. In one instance, on the night of October 20, 1861,

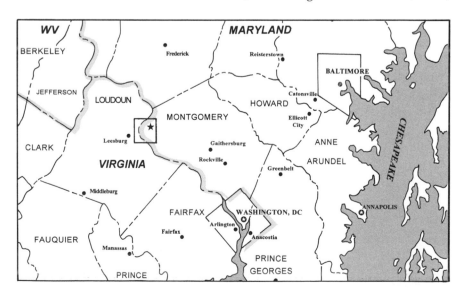

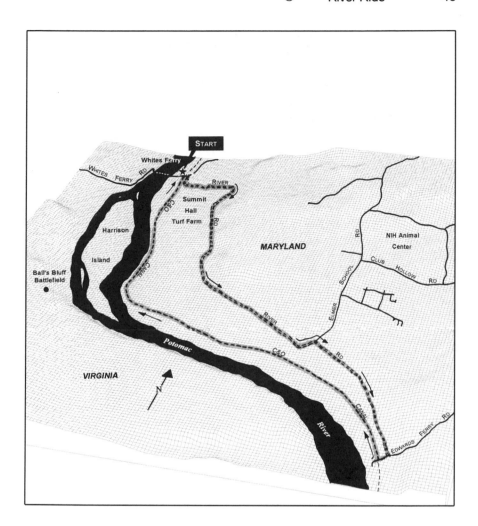

Union troops under General Stone's command at Edwards Ferry and Whites Ferry reported a Confederate camp near Leesburg. In an attempt to intimidate the Confederates into leaving the area, General Stone set in motion events that ultimately resulted in the Battle of Ball's Bluff, costing the Union a severe and gruesome loss. Alternately, Confederate General Jubal A. Early, for whom the present ferry boat at Whites Ferry is named, used both Edwards Ferry and Whites Ferry in retreat after his daring attack on Washington in July 1864.

Today, Whites Ferry is the last of the ferries to carry its customers across the Potomac, operating seven days a week from 6:00 A.M. to 11:00 P.M. In fact, it's the only place between Point of Rocks,

(continued on page 46)

River Ride

☞   **Maryland – From the Capital Beltway** – Take **I-270 North** and go 10.5 miles to **MD-117 west**. Turn **left** at the second stoplight on **MD-124 (Quince Orchard Road)**. Go 2.8 miles on Quince Orchard Road, then make a **right** at the stoplight on **MD-28 (Darnestown Road)**. Bear **left** after 6 miles on **MD-107 (Fisher Avenue then Whites Ferry Road)**. Continue for 11.3 miles to **Whites Ferry** on the Potomac, and park in the **parking lot** on the right.

☞   **Northern Virginia – From the Capital Beltway** – Take Exit 10, **Route 7 west (Leesburg Pike)** all the way to **Leesburg** (22 miles). Just before Leesburg, take **Route 15 (James Monroe Highway)** north. Go approximately 3.5 miles on Route 15, then make a **right** turn on **Whites Ferry Road**. This will take you down to the ferry. You must pay the $2.00 toll and cross the river to park and begin the ride.

MILES   DIRECTIONS

0.0   **START** at the **Whites Ferry parking lot** on the Maryland side of the Potomac River.
Approximately 50 feet north of the parking lot, turn **right** on **RIVER ROAD** (unpaved). This runs parallel to the C&O canal towpath to the right.

3.7   At the three-way intersection, continue **right** on **RIVER ROAD**.

5.2   Turn **right** on **EDWARDS FERRY ROAD**. Cross over the C&O canal and arrive at **Edwards Ferry**.

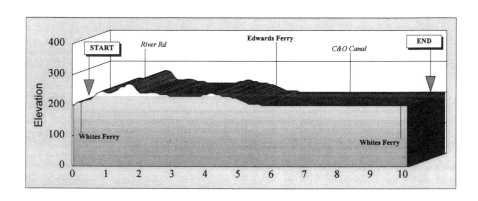

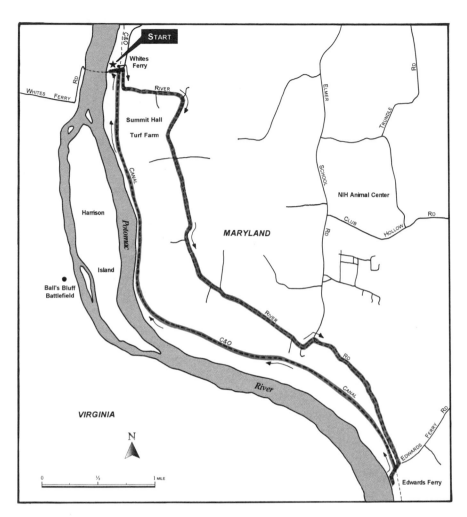

Return along the **C&O TOWPATH** back to **Whites Ferry**.

10.0   Arrive at **Whites Ferry Parking lot**.

Be sure to note the high-water mark on the second story of the Whites Ferry store. The 1972 flood pushed the water level as high as the second story!

(continued from page 43)

Maryland, and the Capital Beltway, to cross the river — a stretch of 40 miles.

As you ride back along the C&O Canal towpath, be sure to notice Harrison Island on your left. During the Civil War, the island served as a temporary hospital to care for the Union's wounded soldiers after their dramatic loss at the battle on Ball's Bluff. One of the wounded taken to Harrison Island was recent Harvard graduate and future Supreme Court Justice, First Lieutenant Oliver Wendell Holmes, Jr. He was shot through the leg and the small of the back, but was diagnosed on the island as "doing well."

This ride, rich in history, is meant for the lighter side of mountain biking, as it travels along flat dirt roads and the C&O Canal towpath. You won't have to worry much about traffic, and should enjoy pedaling past an enormous replica of what many homeowners work a lifetime to achieve — a perfect lawn. The Summit Hall Turf Farm, along River Road, grows a magnificent 380-acre "lawn," carpeted in thick green zoysia, blue grass, bent grass, and mixtures of blue and rye grass. The sod is then harvested and sent to area golf courses, local landscapers, and some very fortunate homeowners.

Ride Information

Trail Maintenance Hotline:

C&O Canal Headquarters	*(301) 739-4200*
Summit Hall Turf Farm	*(301) 948-2900*

Costs:

The ferry is $2.00 per car, 50¢ per bicycle

Maps:

USGS maps:	*Waterford, VA, MD; Poolesville, VA, MD*
	Leesburg, VA, MD; Sterling, VA, MD
ADC maps:	*Montgomery County, MD*

Gen. Jubal A. Early tirelessly ferries its customers across the Potomac

2. Cedarville State Forest

Start: *Park Office*	**Terrain:** *Flat; dirt trails, dirt road*
Length: *8 miles*	**Riding Time:** *45 mins –1 hour*
Rating: *Easy*	**Calories Burned:** *500 – 900*

Here's an off-road ride that rolls along forest roads and wooded trails through Prince George's and Charles Counties' quiet state forest. There are no monuments, natural wonders, or sights of great historical significance in Cedarville State Forest, and even the name may leave you wondering, as cedars are uncommon to the immediate area. (The name, in fact, was taken from a nearby post office.) What this small state forest in southern Maryland does have is a network of wonderful wooded trails and dirt roads to guide you beneath tall stands of loblolly and white pine, around groves of holly and magnolia trees, past a four-acre lake, through the headwaters of Maryland's largest freshwater swamp, and across abandoned farm-land with streams and springs once used for making "moonshine."

The state acquired the land in 1930 during a period of farm abandonment and crop failures in southern Maryland. It planned to use this land to demonstrate techniques in forestry, but now managed it as a place for both recreation and business. You may notice, as you ride through the park, sizeable areas that have been clear cut or thinned. The timber cut, restricted to Virginia and loblolly pine, is

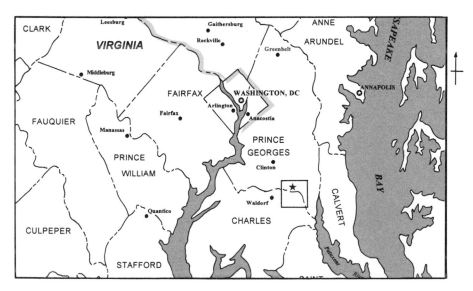

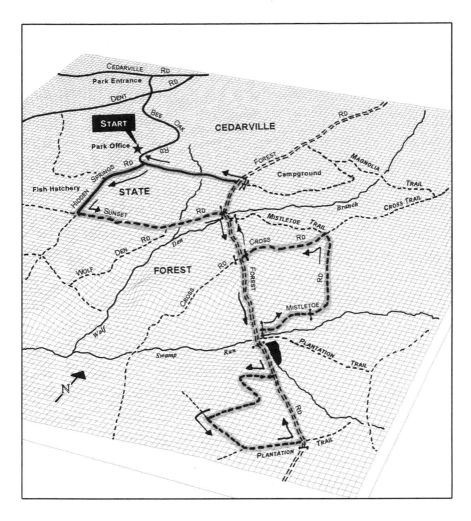

sold to paper mills as far away as West Virginia and Pennsylvania.

This is a great ride for novices and experts alike who have a passion for the great outdoors. Cedarville's terrain is mostly flat, as is most of southern Maryland, but the beauty of its wooded forest roadways rise high above most everything else in the area.

Cedarville State Forest

☞   **From the Capital Beltway (495)** – Exit **South** on **MD-Route 5 (Branch Avenue)** toward **Waldorf**. Go 11.6 miles on MD-Route 5 (joins with US-301), then turn **left** on **Cedarville Road**. Go 2.3 miles, and turn **right** on the forest entrance road **(Bee Oak Road)**. Park Office and parking **1 mile** down the road. No water or telephones. Portable toilets.

MILES   DIRECTIONS

0.0   **START** at **Cedarville State Forest's park office** on Bee Oak **Road**. From the parking lot, turn **right** on **BEE OAK ROAD** (paved).

0.1   Turn **right** on **HIDDEN SPRINGS ROAD** (paved).

0.7   **Hidden Springs Road** comes to an end.   Turn **left** on **SUNSET ROAD**. This is a rolling, rutted dirt trail through the woods (**fish hatchery** to the right at this intersection).

1.7   Turn **right** on **FOREST ROAD** (dirt road).

2.8   Pass **Cedarville Pond** on the left. Go **straight** through the steel gate, continuing on **FOREST ROAD**.

3.1   Turn **right** on **PLANTATION TRAIL (Brown Trail)**, which loops around the south end of the park.

The thick growth of loblolly pine this trail tunnels through

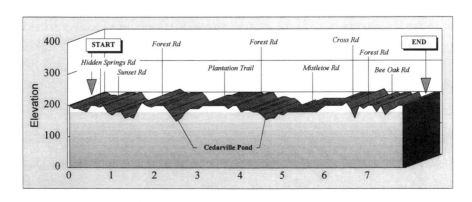

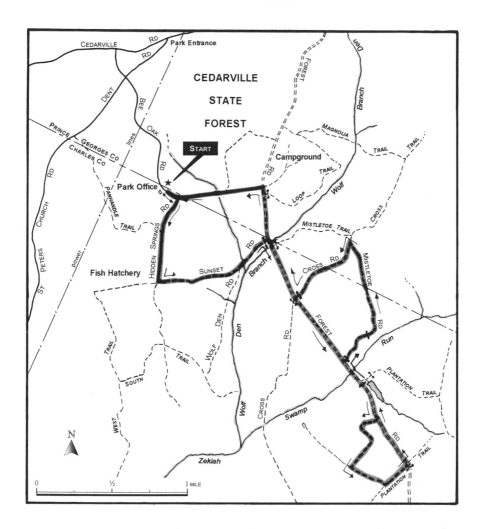

was planted by the Civilian Conservation Corps in the 1930s.

3.6 **PLANTATION TRAIL** comes to a **T**, intersecting with **Swamp Trail (Green Trail)**. Turn **left**, continuing to follow the **Brown Trail** signs.

4.0 Turn **left** on **FOREST ROAD** (dirt road).

4.7 Pass **Cedarville Pond** on the right.

4.8 Turn **right** on **MISTLETOE ROAD** (doubletrack trail).

Watch for the brown, wooden street signs at each intersection along Forest Road.

5.1 Continue **straight** through the wooden gate on **MISTLE-TOE ROAD**.

5.8 Turn **left** on **CROSS ROADS ROAD** at this intersection (doubletrack trail).

5.9 Cross **Heritage Trail**. Continue **Straight** on **CROSS ROADS ROAD**.

6.3 Turn **right** on **FOREST ROAD** (dirt road).

7.2 Turn **left** on **BEE OAK ROAD** (paved).

7.9 Reach the **Park Office**.

Ride Information

Trail Maintenance Hotline:

Maryland Forest, Park, and Wildlife Service

(301) 888-1622

Schedule:

Open every day 8 A.M. to sunset most of the year
Winter schedule, 10 A.M. to sunset

Maps:

USGS maps: *Baltimore, MD; Hughesville, MD*
ADC maps: *Prince George's County road map*
    Charles County road map
Park Service trail map

3. Seneca Creek State Park

Start: *Clopper Lake*	**Terrain:** *Singletrack trails*
Length: *5 miles*	**Riding Time:** *45 mins –1 hour*
Rating: *Easy to moderate*	**Calories Burned:** *500 –1000*

Here's a short but challenging ride around Seneca Creek State Park's Clopper Lake, which will take you along tricky singletrack trails, through undeveloped natural areas, across open fields, around the lake's shores, and past evidence of local history.

You'll begin the ride following the Lake Shore Trail, which crosses old fields and skirts the lake's shoreline. In the spring and summer these fields are filled with colorful wildflowers that give way in the fall to thick, golden sagegrass. Just before the dam you'll be treated to a spectacular view of the lake from King Fisher Overlook. The trail quickly descends across the park road and follows Long Draught Branch, winding up, down, and around beneath a dense canopy of gray birch before crossing the wooded boardwalk to Mink Hollow Trail. Seneca Creek's longest developed trail, Mink Hollow, travels through pine groves and habitats of local wildlife, including white tailed deer. Be careful, though, once you begin the ride along the undeveloped trail edging around the lake. This trail becomes tricky and challenging as exposed roots, steep inclines, occasional flooding, and some quick descents may trip you up if you're not

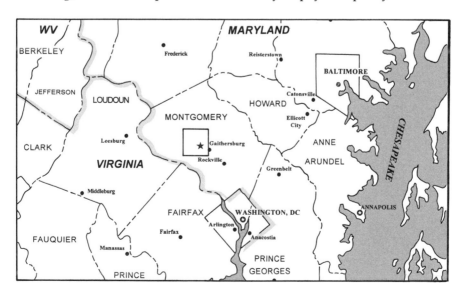

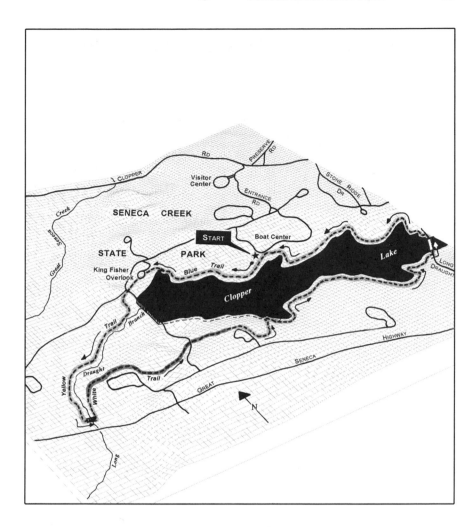

focused.

While Seneca Creek Park extends nearly 13 miles from Gaithersburg south to the Potomac, only this northern section around Clopper Lake is developed for recreation. The lake itself is relatively new, created by damming Long Draught Branch. However, the name "Clopper" has a rich history in this area, dating back to the early 1800s when Francis C. Clopper, a successful tobacco merchant from Philadelphia, purchased more than 540 acres and an existing mill on Seneca Creek. The mill's most prosperous years were between 1830 and 1880, during which time Francis Clopper farmed the land and raised his family. The land remained in the hands of four generations of Clopper's descendants until 1955, when the state purchased the land

(continued on page 59)

Seneca Creek State Park

☞   **From the Capital Beltway (495)** – Take **I-270 north** toward **Frederick**. Just after passing through Gaithersburg on I-270, take the exit for **Route 124 west (Orchard Road)** to **Darnesville**. Follow Route 124 west ½ mile, then turn **right** on **Route 117 (Clopper Road)**. Go 1.5 miles on Clopper Road to the **entrance** to **Seneca Creek State Park on the left**. Follow the **entrance road** into the park. You may park at any of the lots available, including the visitors center, first stop on the right. You may also park at the boat center, but driving the car through the main gate might cost you a small entrance fee.

MILES   DIRECTIONS

0.0   **START** at **Clopper Lake's boat center** (soda machines available). Ride **west** to the end of the circular drive and go straight into the grass on the other side. Follow **LAKE SHORE TRAIL (BLUE)** signs.

0.3   The **LAKE SHORE TRAIL (BLUE)** drops you into an open field. On the other side of this field you will notice the **blue trailhead marker**. Cross the field and continue on **LAKE SHORE TRAIL**. The dam is to the left.

0.5   **LAKE SHORE TRAIL (BLUE)** brings you right up to **King Fisher Overlook**. You can catch a nice view of the lake from here.

Follow the remainder of the **BLUE TRAIL**, which reenters the woods at the back side of the circular drive. Go down

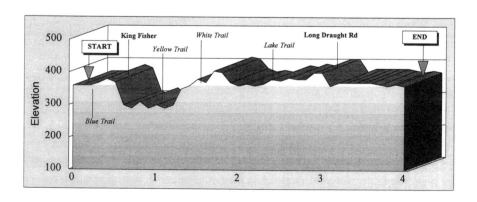

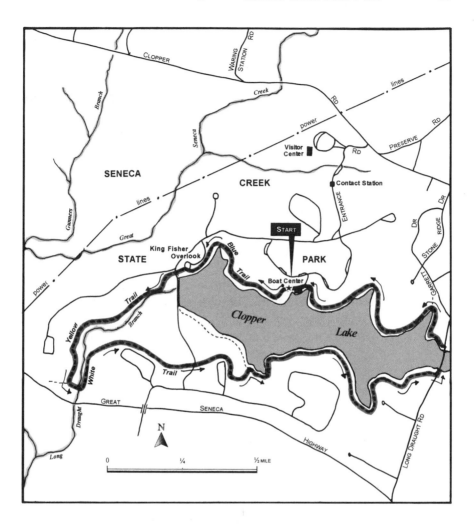

the little hill through the woods and immediately cross the road.

0.55 **LONG DRAUGHT TRAIL (YELLOW)** begins catty-corner to where the **Blue Trail** ends.

1.1 Turn **left** on **MINK HOLLOW TRAIL (WHITE)**.

1.2 Bear **left**, continuing on **MINK HOLLOW TRAIL (WHITE)** over a narrow boardwalk, crossing the creek.

1.8 Cross the park road. Continue **straight** on the **WHITE TRAIL**.

2.2   **Mink Hollow Trail (white)** comes to the lake. Turn **right**, following the trail around the lake.

3.4   This trail zips up on **Long Draught Road**. Cross **Long Draught Road** on the **asphalt path**. Once you're across the bridge, turn **left** through the guardrail and back on the trail around the lake.

3.7   This trail drops you down to a flat, **gravel path**. Turn **right**. (Turning left takes you to a dead-end at the lake.) Stay right on this gravel path for about 20 feet. Then turn **left** across the creek to hook up with the path that continues to follow the perimeter of the lake.

4.3   Turn **left**, crossing over a little wooden bridge at the end of the alcove. Continue following the trail.

4.7   Arrive at the boat center and grab a soda from the soda machine. What a ride!

Ride Information

Trail Maintenance Hotline:

Maryland Forest, Park, and Wildlife Service

(301) 924-2127

Schedule:

Park is open every day
April through September, 8 A.M. to dusk
October through March, 10 A.M. to dusk

Maps:

USGS maps: Germantown, MD; Gaithersburg, MD
ADC maps: Montgomery County
Seneca Creek State Park trail map

(continued from page 55)

and added it to Seneca Creek State Park.

Throughout the park there is evidence of the past – abandoned farms and old meadows now covered by new growth, traces of some of Clopper's old mills, and many of Clopper's old farm lanes. Mill ruins can still be seen from the intersection of Clopper Road and Waring Station Road, just west of the park entrance, and traces of the Clopper home are evident near the visitors center.

Please be aware, as always, that many other outdoor enthusiasts share these same trails. Always yield the right of way to any other trail users, and ride cautiously since the trails have many hidden turns and difficult negotiations.

4. Mckeldin Area

Start: *Switchback trailhead*	**Terrain:** *Hard dirt/singletrack trails*
Length: *5 miles*	**Riding Time:** *45 mins – 1 hour*
Rating: *Easy to moderate*	**Calories Burned:** *600 – 1000*

Switchback Trail through the Mckeldin Area is the perfect example of a "classic ride" if there ever was one. It begins as a well-maintained, packed-dirt and gravel trail all the way to the river. Along the way, serene forested surroundings isolate you from the hectic Washington grind, transporting you deep into a peaceful wilderness. Once you reach the picturesque south branch of the Patapsco River, Switchback Trail becomes a fun and challenging singletrack, rugged, yet well maintained. Nearing the end of the ride, after a respite along the river's banks, you are confronted with the ultimate challenge as the trail turns sharply left and goes vertical. There are no ways around it, and even walking up can be a task. This is not to say that riding up is not possible, however, and I issue this challenge to anyone willing to go for it!

The Mckeldin Area is a unique stop along the Patapsco Valley State Park, nudged into the southeast corner of Carroll County where the North Branch and the South Branch of the Patapsco River converge. Liberty Lake, one of Baltimore's primary water supplies, fills the valley just north of Mckeldin. Liberty Lake was created by

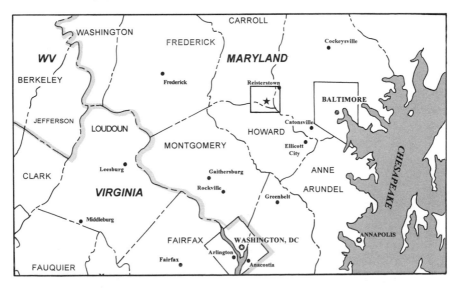

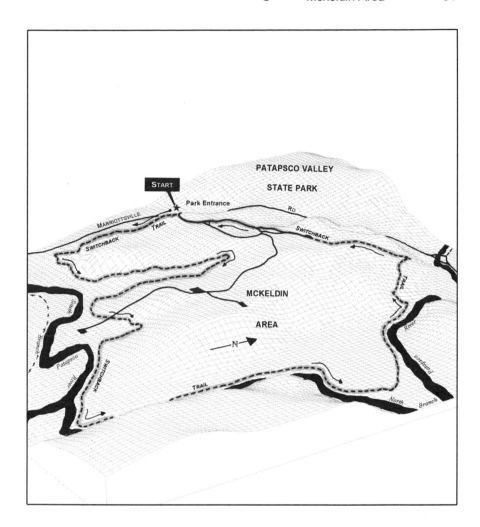

damming the North Branch less than one mile from Switchback Trail.

Switchback Trail is open to hikers, bikers, and equestrians alike and is popular throughout the year. Fortunately, the trail's design is well suited for all those wishing to enjoy its delightful scenery. But please take caution when riding the same trails with horseback riders and hikers. The park is filled with blind corners and quick turns, and a sudden run-in with a horse may be the perfect opportunity for disaster.

Mckeldin Area

☞   **From the Baltimore Beltway (695)** – Take **I-70 west**. Go 8.5 miles to **Exit 83 Marriottsville Road north**. Follow Marriottsville Road north for 4 miles, passing through Marriottsville. The **Mckeldin Area** park entrance road is on the right. Turn **right** on the **park entrance road,** and follow it uphill to the parking area.

MILES   DIRECTIONS

0.0   **START** from the main entrance road at the information/toll booth.

The trailhead is just off the road with a clearly marked sign that reads **"Switchback Trail, 5 miles."** You will follow this **white blazed** trail the entire way through the park.

0.5   Come to the end of the descent.

0.6   At the fork in the trail, stay **left**, following the much larger **SWITCHBACK TRAIL**. Climb for about 0.2 miles. The trail then changes to rolling terrain.

1.2   Pass a small shelter on the right and a minor trail turning left up to the ballfield. Stay **right**, continuing on **SWITCHBACK TRAIL**.

1.6   Come to the end of another good descent.   Stay **left**, continuing on **SWITCHBACK TRAIL**.

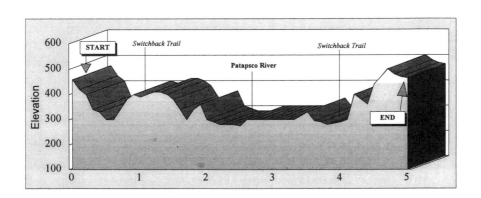

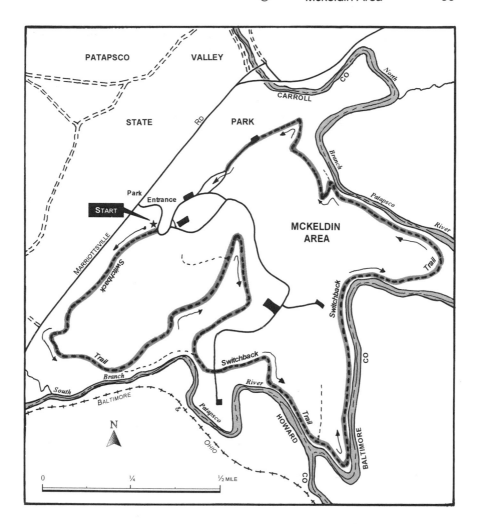

1.8 Cross the paved **park road**. **SWITCHBACK TRAIL** picks up directly across the road and changes to all singletrack. It follows some difficult rollers before racing all the way downhill to the Patapsco River.

2.0 Reach the bottom of the descent. At the river, turn **left** on **SWITCHBACK TRAIL**, riding downstream with the river.

3.0 Stay **right**, continuing along the North Branch River.

3.9 Turn **hard left** away from the river and attempt to ride straight up this vertical climb.

4.0   Reach the top of the hill. Turn **right**, continuing to follow the **WHITE BLAZE** at the top. Note the wooden trail post here.

4.4   Reach the asphalt road. Follow this all the way back around to the parking area.

5.0   Reach the **parking lot**.

Ride Information

Trail Maintenance Hotline:

Patapsco Valley State Park HQ   *(410) 461-5005*
Emergency 24 hrs   *(410) 461-0050*
TTD   *(301) 974-3683*

Costs:

$2.00 on weekends and holidays

Schedule:

Open from 10 A.M. to sunset, Thursday – Sunday

Maps:

USGS maps: Sykesville, MD
ADC maps: Carroll County, Baltimore County road maps
Patapsco Valley State Park trail map

Horseback riding along the Patapsco River

5. Patuxent River Park

Start: *Park Office*	**Terrain:** *Singletrack*
Length: *7 miles*	**Riding Time:** *1 hour*
Rating: *Easy to moderate*	**Calories Burned:** *600 – 1000*

The ride through this section of the Patuxent River Park is a fantastic journey over its wooded, rolling terrain on nearly 10 miles of woodland horse trails and singletrack. The trails, open to hikers, horseback riders, and cyclists, lead you through Jug Bay's beautiful 2,000-acre "limited-use natural area," and provide a close-up look at a coastal ecosystem in one of Maryland's premier greenways.

Acquired by the Maryland Department of Natural Resources, the Jug Bay Natural Area represents the nationally acclaimed land preservation program of the state of Maryland called Program Open Space. This program was designed to preserve open-space land and to protect valuable natural resources.

The results of this program offer something of value to all who come and visit. Naturalists are given the unique opportunity to observe freshwater, tidal, and nontidal wetlands; historians may exhibit life along the river during the nineteenth century at The Patuxent Village; nature lovers can drive a four-mile, self-guided tour through the Merkle Wildlife Sanctuary, including the thousand-foot boardwalk crossing the Mattaponi Creek; hunters enjoy bow season

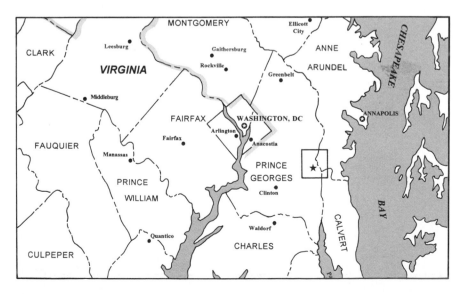

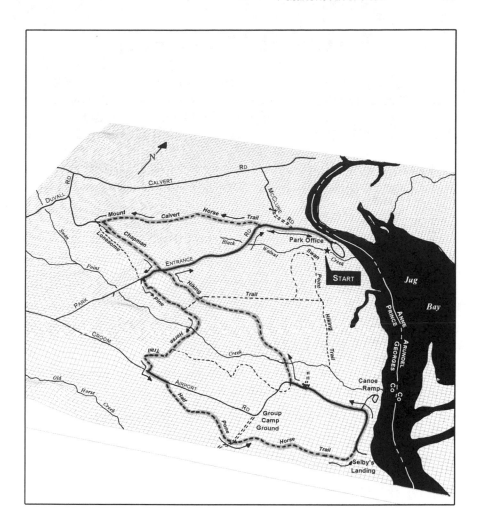

for squirrel, rabbit, and deer; hikers and equestrians have miles of trails; and, of course, off-road bicyclists are welcome. All hikers and riders, though, are required to register at the park office and obtain a park permit before venturing onto its trails. Permits can be obtained at the start of this ride from the park office for $2.00 a visit. A seasonal visitors pass is also available.

This fabulous ride offers cyclists wanting to venture off the road and into the woods a fantastic opportunity to see nature up close without the grueling pressures of steep climbs and treacherous descents. Don't be fooled, though. Patuxent River Park is full of exciting trails to keep cyclists of any ability interested and entertained.

Patuxent River Park

☞   **From the Capital Beltway (495)** – Take **Exit 11 east** on **Route 4 east (Pennsylvania Avenue)**. Follow Route 4 east (Pennsylvania Avenue) 6.3 miles, then **exit left** on **Old Crain Highway south**. Almost immediately, turn **left** on **Croom Station Road**. Go 2.5 miles and turn **left** on **Croom Road (Route 382)**. Go 1.3 miles and turn **left** on **Croom Airport Road**. This takes you into **Patuxent River Park**. After 2 miles turn **left** on **Park Entrance Road** and travel 1.5 miles to the end, parking at the **park office.**

MILES   DIRECTIONS

0.0   **START** from the **Park Office** at the northern end of **Park Entrance Road**. Travel **south** on **PARK ENTRANCE ROAD**.

0.4   Turn **right** off Park Entrance Road through a wooden gate to **MOUNT CALVERT HORSE TRAIL**. The trail is slightly hidden from the road. A wooden post with a horse-trail symbol marks the trailhead.

1.2   Turn **left** on **CHAPMAN HIKING TRAIL**. This trail leads you away from a field into the woods.

1.6   Exit the woods around a steel gate and turn **right** on **PARK ENTRANCE ROAD**. Look for the **yellow horse x-ing sign** just up the road.

1.7   Turn **left** on the **LONESOME PINE HORSE TRAIL** just

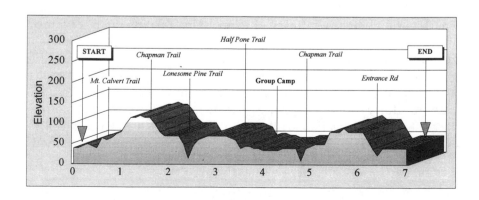

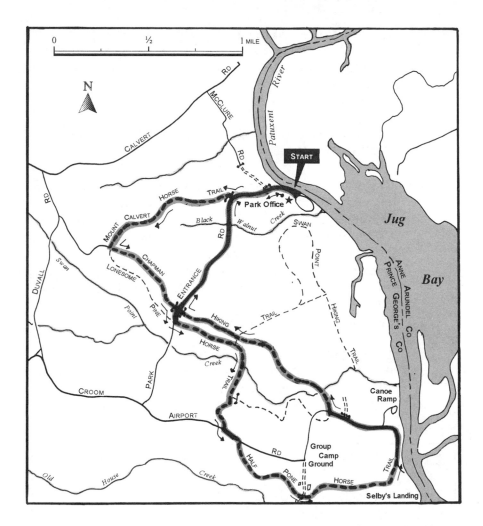

past the **yellow horse x-ing sign**. This trail is marked by a wooden post with the horse trail symbol on it.

2.0 Turn **right** at this trail intersection, continuing downhill. Be careful of the wooden water bars laid across the trail.

2.3 Turn **right** at this trail intersection, continuing on the **LONESOME PINE HORSE TRAIL**. Turning left takes you on a hilly ride along another horse trail to Croom Airport Road. This trail is often closed during wet seasons.

2.6 Turn **left** on **CROOM AIRPORT ROAD**. You should see the **yellow horse x-ing sign** to the left up the road. Keep your eyes open for this trail.

2.7   Turn **right** on the **HALF PONE HORSE TRAIL**. This trail is a bit obscure. Keep your eyes open for the wooden post that marks it.

3.2   Cross the dirt jeep trail, continuing straight on **HALF PONE HORSE TRAIL**.

3.5   Cross another dirt road. Follow **HALF PONE HORSE TRAIL** along the perimeter of the **group campgrounds**. The campgrounds and picnic area should be on your left. Continue following the trail around the **right** side of the corn fields. You will continue along what seems to be a tractor path around the corn fields until it dumps you back on **Croom Airport Road** next to **Selby's Landing** boat ramp.

4.6   Pass the gravel road and gate on the right.

4.9   Turn **right** off **Croom Airport Road** back into the woods on the **HORSE TRAIL**. This trailhead is very obscure and overgrown. It begins down off the road behind the weeds and is marked by a **wooden horse trail post**. There is a post

Ride Information

Trail Maintenance Hotline:

   Patuxent River Park   *(301) 627-6074*

Costs:

   Required **park-use permit** *(available at park office)*
   You may purchase a seasonal visitors pass — or — pay $2.00 a visit

Schedule:

   Open daily from 8 A.M. until dusk with seasonal adjustments
   Park office is open from 8 A.M. to 4 P.M.

Maps:

     USGS maps: Bristol, MD
     ADC maps: Prince George's road map
     Dept. of Parks & Recreation trail map
     Patuxent River Park trail map

on opposite sides of Croom Airport Road at this point.

5.7   Reach the trail intersection and continue **straight**.

6.0   Turn **right** on **PARK ENTRANCE ROAD**. You can, of course, go straight on the hiking trail if you like.

7.0   Arrive back at the **Park Office**. Get a drink and ride down to Jug Bay for some rest.

6. L.F. Cosca Regional Park

Start: *Clearwater Nature Center* **Terrain:** *Singletrack*

Length: *5+ miles of trails* **Riding Time:** *30 mins – 1 hour*

Rating: *Easy to moderate* **Calories Burned:** *300 – 1000*

Some things in life can often deceive you, disappoint you, then leave you feeling shortchanged. Louise F. Cosca Regional Park, just outside the town of Clinton in Prince George's County, Maryland, is one such place that will, indeed, deceive you. It will not, however, leave you disappointed. Despite its small size, this park has everything an off-road cyclist can dream of — deep, wooded surroundings, stream crossings, a beautiful 15-acre lake, tough singletrack trails, and a variety of route possibilities.

You'll start from the parking lot of Clearwater Nature Center, one of the state's most unique and innovative nature centers. This lava-rock building is placed deep within the woods, featuring a large greenhouse, indoor pond, and living creatures of the forest. From here, you'll descend quickly into the woods onto the park's main trail. (Although this book guides you left around the perimeter of the park, don't hesitate to explore and create your own circuits.) The trail travels quickly along the creek, often precariously close to the water's edge, then up through the trees above the creek valley. This, of course, leads to a thrilling, narrow descent down a winding single-

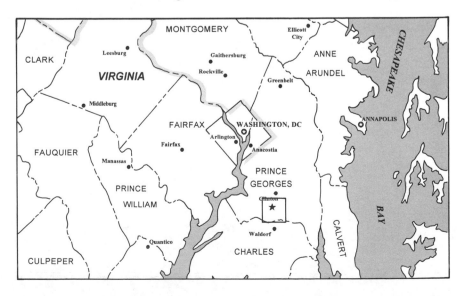

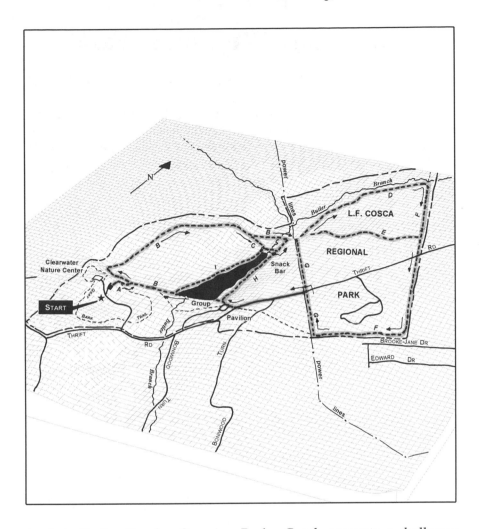

track to Butler Creek. Crossing Butler Creek presents a challenge though, because it is a bit too wide to jump and somewhat difficult to negotiate from the bike. While descending the last hill, detour right onto "Trail C" and take the easy route over the creek via a small wooden bridge at the north end of the lake. Once across the creek, the trails twist back and forth beneath tall oak, chestnut, and birch, which, in the late autumn, are breathtaking. Continuing around the perimeter of the park, the trails roll more gently back toward the start of the ride, allowing you to sit back and enjoy your colorful surroundings.

The variety of possible routes within Cosca's 500 acres of rolling, wooded parkland will turn your ride into much more than a

(continued on page 77)

L.F. Cosca Regional Park

☞   **From the Capital Beltway (495)** – Take **Exit 7** to **MD-Route 5 South (Branch Avenue)** toward **Waldorf**. Go approximately 4 miles to **Route 223 (Woodyard Road)**. Turn **right** on **Woodyard Road**, taking this 0.6 miles to **Brandywine Road**. Turn **left** on **Brandywine Road**. Follow this south toward **Clinton** 0.75 miles, then turn **right** on **Thrift Road**. Thrift Road takes you south 1.5 miles to the **park entrance** on your **right**. Go **right** into the park to the **Clearwater Nature Center** on top of the hill. Parking, telephone, toilets, and small creatures at the nature center.

MILES   DIRECTIONS

0.0   **START** from the parking lot at the **Clearwater Nature Center** and follow **TRAIL A** down wooden-plank steps into the woods.

0.1   Turn **left** at this trail intersection with **Trail B**. Turning right takes you along a secondary trail toward the Group Pavilion. Straight on Trail B leads you up a steep hill to the lake.

0.8   You may either continue **straight** on **Trail B** down this fantastic descent **or** turn **right** on **Trail C,** then **left** on **Trail H**. The strategy is to connect with **Trail D**.

The advantage of detouring on Trail C, then left on Trail H back to Trail D, is that you avoid slogging through thick brush and Butler Branch Creek, over which there is no solid place to cross. Take your pick.

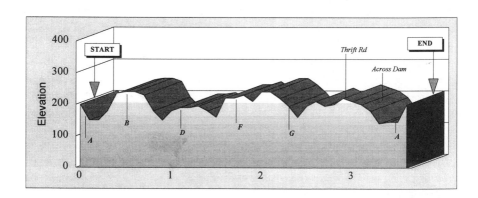

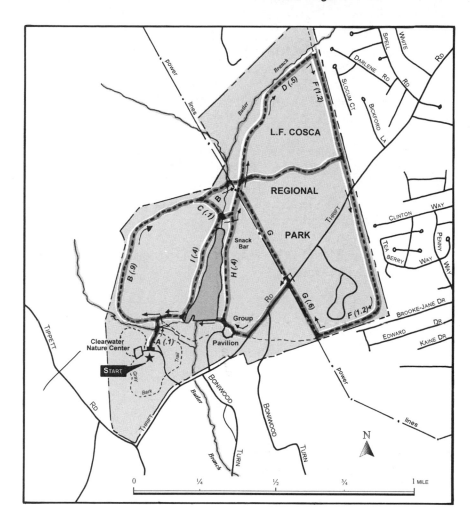

1.0   Bear **left** on **TRAIL D**. This is an exciting trail, taking you up and down on a quick and challenging singletrack.

Trail E is a fun alternative here, twisting quickly through the woods along a more level terrain.

1.5   Turn **right** on **TRAIL F**. This trail gently rolls along a more open jeep trail.

2.0   Cross Thrift Road. Continue on **TRAIL F**.

2.7   Turn **right** at the **POWER LINES (Trail G)**.

2.9   Turn **left** on **THRIFT ROAD**. You could follow the power lines (Trail G) all the way back into the park.

3.1   Bear **right** off Thrift Road to a **HIKING TRAIL**, which takes you past the Group Pavilion and up to the dam.

3.3   Reach the lake. Cross the dam, taking **TRAIL B** down the hill back to Trail A.

A good diversion at the lake — turn **right** to the **snack bar** for some food.

3.5   Follow **TRAIL A** back up the hill to the **Clearwater Nature Center** parking lot.

Ride Information

Trail Maintenance Hotline:

L.F. Cosca Regional Park	*(301) 868-1397*
Clearwater Nature Center	*(301) 297-4575*

Costs:

Memorial Day to Labor Day, nonresidents of Prince George's or Montgomery Co. must pay a $5.00 parking fee for parking within the confines of the park.

Schedule:

Open daily 7:30 A.M. to dusk, year-round.

Maps:

USGS maps: Piscataway, MD
ADC maps: Prince George's road map
Park Service trail map

Hoppin' logs on one of Cosca's great trails

(continued from page 73)

quick jaunt through the woods. You can spend hours exploring the different trails, then pedal over to the snack bar and finish a great day of riding by lounging along the shorelines of the lake.

7. Greenbelt/Northeast Branch

Start: *Greenbelt Lake*	**Terrain:** *Flat, asphalt/dirt trails*
Length: *23.3 miles round trip*	**Riding Time:** *1½ – 2 hours*
Rating: *Moderate*	**Calories Burned:** *900 – 1500*

The Northeast Branch Hiker-Biker-Equestrian Trail offers access to a number of places, including the University of Maryland at College Park, Greenbelt Lake and Greenbelt Park, College Park Airport, beautiful Lake Artemesia, Anacostia River Park, and the Dueling Branch Natural Area.

Much of this ride follows the Northeast Branch Hiker-Biker-Equestrian Trail on flat, paved paths through Prince George's urban environment. The pavement ends just past Riverdale Road, and you must travel atop a series of earthen dikes stretching along either side of the Northeast Branch to the Anacostia River Park. These dikes take you past the town of Riverdale, then through the village of Bladensburg, once a battlefield in the War of 1812.

Rising abruptly almost 85 feet above the Anacostia River, absent of trees, and emitting harmless traces of methane gas, you will recognize the Anacostia River Park. The park was designed in the 1970s by the Maryland-National Capital Park and Planning Commission to include football and baseball fields, basketball courts, and a hiker-biker trail. First, however, the Commission needed to truck in

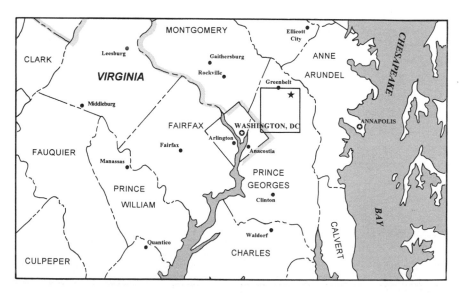

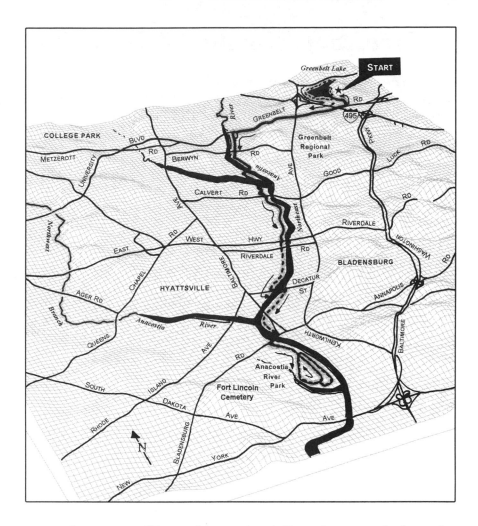

as much as two million cubic yards of dirt, taken mostly from the excavated Metro tunnels, to blanket more than a million tons of garbage piled in what was the former Anacostia Landfill. The Maryland-National Capital Park and Planning Commission later added the Dueling Branch Natural Area, which takes you by dirt road along a scenic loop through the area's natural habitats.

On a ride through an urban setting such as this, there is undoubtedly a good deal of interesting things to see along the way. Greenbelt, for example, was once a farming community, but became part of an experiment by the federal government in the early 1900s to create a completely self-sufficient community. These "garden towns" would have their own government, schools, shopping areas, and

(continued on page 83)

Greenbelt/Northeast Branch

☞   **From the Capital Beltway (495)** – Take **Exit 23** to **Kenilworth Avenue south.** Imediately turn **left** on **Greenbelt Road (Route 193)**, and go three-fourths of a mile to **Lakecrest Drive**. Turn **left** on **Lakecrest Drive** toward **Greenbelt Lake**. The entrance to the bike path around the lake is on the right, about one-half mile from Greenbelt Road.

MILES   DIRECTIONS

0.0   **START** at the **Greenbelt Lake** entrance on **Lakecrest Drive** and follow the **bike trail signs** to the **GRAVEL TRAIL** circling the lake.   Stay **right**, riding **counterclockwise** around the lake.

1.6   Exit the **gravel trail** around Greenbelt Lake and turn **left** on **LAKECREST DRIVE**.   Follow the green bike trail signs toward **Greenbelt Road**.

1.9   Turn **right** on the **GREENBELT ROAD STATE BIKEWAY**. This is simply a designated bikeway on the shoulder of Greenbelt Road.

4.1   Turn **left** on **57th AVENUE**.   Immediately turn **right** on **NORTHEAST BRANCH HIKER BIKER EQUESTRIAN TRAIL**.   Indian Creek is on your right.

4.5   Cross **Berwyn Road**.

5.1   Turn hard **right** on the **wooden foot bridge** over Indian

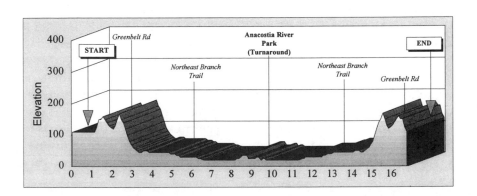

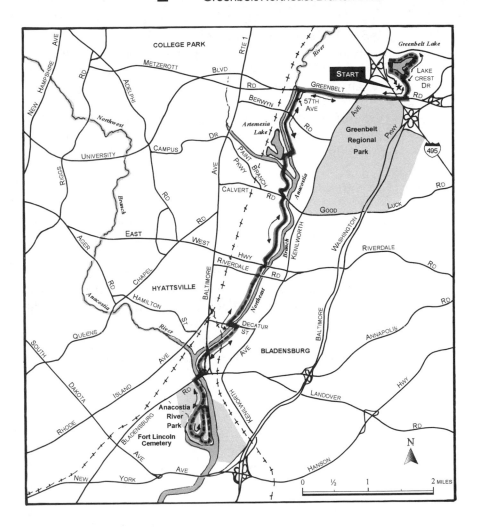

Creek. Indian Creek should now be on your left. The entrance to Lake Artesmesia is directly in front of you. Turn **left** to continue following the **NORTHEAST BRANCH TRAIL**.

5.7 Pass **College Park Airport**.

5.9 Cross **Calvert Road**.

6.7 Pass the **Riverdale Recreation Center** on the right. Water here.

7.2 Go underneath **East West Highway,** then cross over

Riverdale Road. The asphalt path ends here. Once across Riverdale Road, trailblaze straight across to the **levee** and, riding atop the **LEVEE**, travel downstream. The Northeast Branch creek is on the left.

8.0   Turn **left** and cross over the **DECATUR STREET BRIDGE**. Continue downstream atop the levee. The creek is now on your right.

8.4   Cross the railroad tracks.

8.6   Cross **Route 1, Baltimore Avenue**. Continue following the **LEVEE** south toward Bladensburg Road.

9.0   Turn **right** on **BLADENSBURG ROAD**, crossing the bridge over the river. Once across the bridge, take an immediate **left** on an unmarked road on the right side of the Anacostia River. This road takes you into the Anacostia River Park.

9.3   Road changes to dirt. Follow this rutted road counterclockwise around the base of the park.

10.5   The rutted park road appears to end. Detour **right** down

Ride Information

Trail Maintenance Hotline:

Maryland-National Capital Park and Planning Commission
Trail Maintenance line – (301) 952-3522
National Park Service   (301) 426-6975

Schedule:

Open daily from dawn until dusk, year-round

Maps:

USGS maps: Beltsville, MD; Washington East, DC, MD
ADC maps: Prince George's County road map
Park Service trail map

into the woods through a steel gate. The sign at this gate
reads **Anacostia River Park/Dueling Creek Natural Area**.
Follow this dirt road through the natural area. There are a
few places to stop and enjoy different points of interest
within the natural area.

11.6   Arrive back at the **Dueling Creek Natural Area** entrance
gate. Follow the road back to Bladensburg Road.

12.0   After looping through the River Park, arrive back at
Bladensburg Road.

At this point, return the way you came, back to Greenbelt
Lake.

cs

(continued from page 79)

open land. They were intended to provide affordable housing and act
as a buffer between the cities and suburbs, maintaining the open
countryside. While this idea never firmly took hold, the National Park
Service maintained some of the land and turned it into parkland.
Greenbelt Park was one such area. Once farmland, a second-growth
forest has emerged in Greenbelt Park and is now one of Washington's
wonderful suburban parks.

Further down the trail you'll cross over Decatur St., named for
Commodore Stephen Decatur, the Tripolitan War hero, killed in a
duel on March 22, 1820. Dueling was not an isolated event in this area
during the nineteenth century, as more than 50 duels were fought just
upstream from Dueling Branch Creek. The name, of course, comes
from the grounds where these "notables" settled their disputes.

Once you reach the Anacostia River Park, look south past
Dueling Branch to the high hill now occupied by Lincoln Cemetery.
This hill was once the post of a small American militia positioned there
to help defend Washington against British soldiers during the War of
1812. The British, however, had little trouble getting by, marching
into Washington and burning the Capitol and the president's house.

The ride, round trip, is just over 23 miles. You may not wish
to ride the whole distance back to the start, in which case you will need
to arrange for a car to shuttle you back.

8. Northern Central Rail Trail

Start: *Ashland parking lot*	**Terrain:** *Flat, hard-packed dirt trail*
Length: *19.7 miles one way*	**Riding Time:** *1 – 2 hours*
Rating: *Moderate*	**Calories Burned:** *1000 – 2000*

Back when rails were king, the Northern Central Railroad was among the few rail lines dominating the Mid-Atlantic, carrying everything from milk and coal to the U.S. Mail and U.S. Presidents. For nearly 134 years the Northern Central Railroad was the locomotive link that carved its way through Maryland's hilly Piedmont region and Pennsylvania's rolling farmlands, connecting Baltimore with Gettysburg, York, and Harrisburg.

Scores of small towns sprang up along the line to prosper from Northern Central's service to the cities. Towns such as Freeland, Bentley Springs, Parkton, Whitehall, Monkton, Corbett, Phoenix, and Ashland sent their flour, milk, paper, coal, textiles, and other goods to Baltimore, and thrived along the railroad's route.

The Northern Central also served in the Civil War, carrying wounded soldiers south to Baltimore hospitals from the bloody battlefields of Gettysburg. Abraham Lincoln rode the Northern Central north to Gettysburg to deliver his famous Gettysburg Address. It later carried his body back through Gettysburg on an agonizing trip to be buried, following his assassination on April 14,

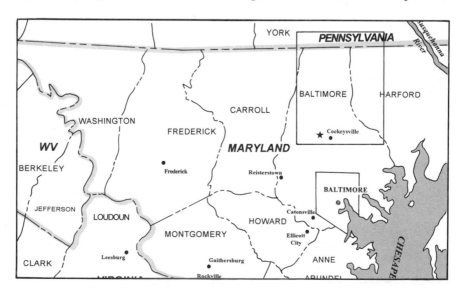

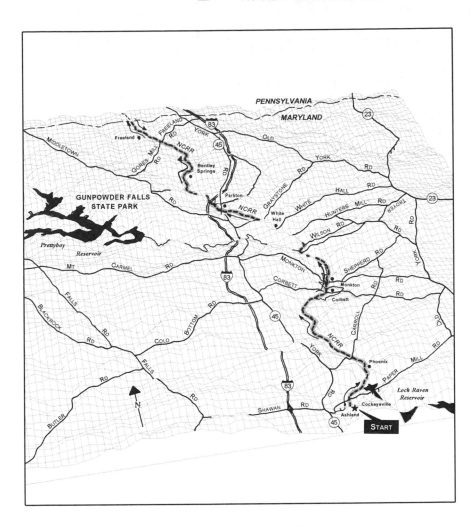

1865, at Ford's Theater in Washington, D.C.

The rail's rich history began to recede with the advent of trucks and automobiles, and in 1959 the Northern Central had to give up its local passenger service. But it was Agnes, the powerful hurricane of 1972, that dealt the final blow to the faltering rail line when it washed out and destroyed many of the railroad's bridges, ultimately knocking out remaining main-line passenger services and the line's important freight transportation. Northern Central Railroad's commercial success ended, but its new identity and prosperity were just beginning.

The rail line south of Cockeysville was purchased by the state of Maryland for freight service, which left the remaining line from Cockeysville north to the Pennsylvania border open for a unique and

(continued on page 89)

Northern Central Rail Trail

☞   **From the Baltimore Beltway (695)** – Take **I-83 North** 5.5 miles to **Exit 20 (Shawan Road)**. Go east on **Shawan Road** less than 1 mile, then turn **right** on **Route 45 (York Road)**. Go 1 mile and turn **left** on **Ashland Road**. Follow **Ashland Road** 1.5 miles, passing **Hunt Valley Shopping Center** on your left. Stay **right** on Ashland Road toward the **parking lot** for the **Northern Central Railroad Trail**. (Do not bear left on Paper Mill Road.)

MILES   DIRECTIONS

0.0   **START** from the **NCRR Trail parking lot** in **Ashland** and travel north on the **Northern Central Railroad Trail**.

2.0   Pass through the town of Phoenix. Toilets, telephone, parking on the left.

Sight of the Phoenix textile mill razed for Loch Raven Reservoir. The reservoir, when built in 1922, never reached the mill. The mill ruins exist today, and are still above the water line.

4.0   Pass through the town of Sparks.

6.0   Pass through the historic Victorian village of Corbett. Listed on the National Registry of Historic Places.

7.5   Pass through Monkton, showcasing the renovated Monkton train station, now a museum and park office. Monkton is

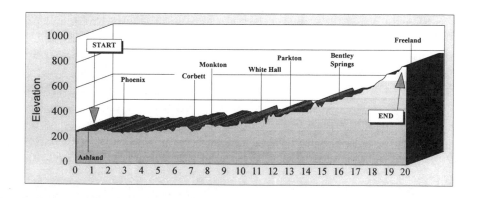

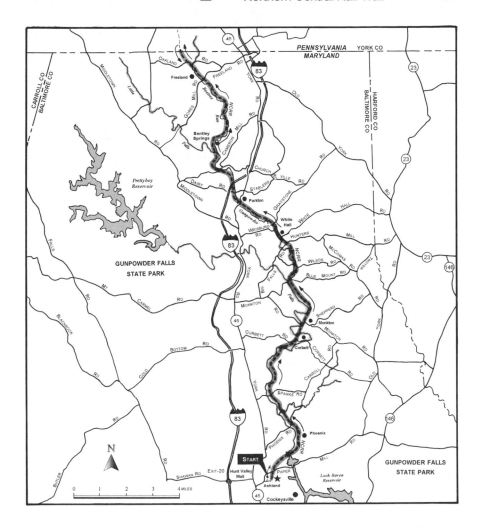

also listed on the National Registry of Historic Places. Restroom, telephones, and food available. Bike rental and repair shop just off the main path.

10.8 Pass through the village of Whitehall. Telephones and parking on the left. Whitehall is a former paper mill town that used the rail to export its paper to Baltimore.

12.9 Pass through Parkton. Parkton was the railroad's hub for exporting dairy products south to Baltimore.

15.7 Reach the historic resort town of Bentley Springs. Portable toilet available.

18.0   Pass through the town of Freeland. Restrooms and parking available.

19.7   Reach the Maryland-Pennsylvania state border.

From here, you should either have arranged for a car to shuttle you back to the Ashland parking lot, or you must ride back under your own pedaling power.

Ride Information

Trail Maintenance Hotline:

Gunpowder Falls State Park	*(301) 592-2897*
Rails-to-Trails Conservancy	*(202) 797-5400*

Maps:

USGS maps:	*Cockeysville, MD; Hereford, MD*
	Phoenix, MD; New Freedom, MD
ADC maps:	*Baltimore County road map*

Also Available:

Guide to the Northern Central Railroad Trail
*$6.50 (postpaid) from Howling Wolf Publications
8630 Fenton St., Silver Spring, MD 20910
(301) 589-9455*

Fletcher Harris

Crossing Gunpowder Falls

(continued from page 85)

wonderful opportunity. This opportunity was realized by the residents of Baltimore County in 1980 when they purchased the 20-mile corridor from Penn Central and began the back-breaking process of converting the rails to trails. After nine long, hard years of work and thousands of volunteer hours later, the Northern Central Trail from Ashland to the Pennsylvania border was finished.

Now more than 180,000 people visit the trail each year. The Northern Central Trail carries its visitors across Maryland's beautiful fields and meadows, past old forests and rural farmland, along the rushing waters of Little Falls and Gunpowder Falls, and through the many historic towns whose histories are based on the corridor between Baltimore with Harrisburg called the Northern Central.

Be warned that this once-quiet treasure is gaining tremendous popularity and parking is very limited during the prime outdoor months. Take this into account when you wish to travel the rail, and be sure to get there early.

9. Sugarloaf's Scenic Circuit

Start: *Sugarloaf park entrance* **Terrain:** *Paved/unpaved roads*
Length: *12 miles* **Riding Time:** *1 – 1½ hours*
Rating: *Moderate* **Calories Burned:** *900 – 1500*

Named after the sugarloaf by early pioneers because of its shape, Sugarloaf Mountain stands at an elevation of 1282 feet, more than 800 feet above the Monocacy Valley. The mountain dominates the landscape for miles and has attracted its share of attention throughout history. The earliest known map of Sugarloaf was sketched by a Swiss explorer in 1707 while the U.S. was still part of the colonies of Britain. It is noted that General Braddock marched past the mountain in 1775 during the French and Indian War. The mountain later became a matter of contention between the North and South during the Civil War, as its summit and overlooks provided ideal observation of the valleys below.

During the very early part of the twentieth century the mountain's main peak and surrounding land was purchased by Gordon Strong who in 1946 organized Stronghold, Incorporated, a nonprofit organization designed for "enjoyment and education in an appreciation of natural beauty." Strong's original intent was a vacation retreat. He built the Strong Mansion atop the mountain and a number of homes at the foot of the mountain in what is now

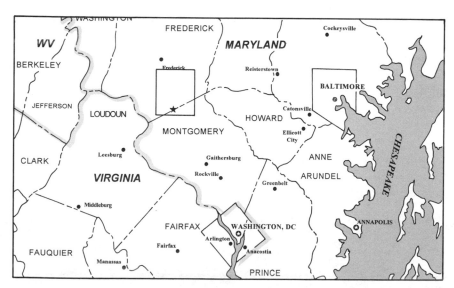

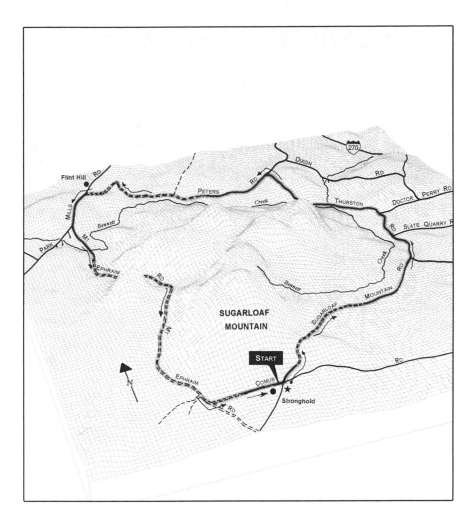

Stronghold. Since Strong's death in 1954, Stronghold, Inc., has continued to manage the 3,250 acres of land on and around Sugarloaf Mountain as a place of natural beauty and wildlife, committed to maintaining its natural state.

This loop travels on both paved and unpaved roads surrounding Sugarloaf Mountain, which is always looming above you as you pedal past magnificent horse farms and along the rushing waters of Bennett Creek. This is not a ride recommended for a regular road bike, since many roads are gravel and dirt. As you climb back over the mountain toward Stronghold on Mount Ephraim Road, all remnants of pavement disappear and you are transported deep into a mountain forest.

(continued on page 94)

Sugarloaf's Scenic Cicuit

☞   **From the Capital Beltway (495)** – Take **I-270 north** approximately 21 miles to the **Hyattstown exit (Exit 22)**. Circle under I-270, heading southwest on **Route 109 (Old Hundred Road)**. Follow **Old Hundred Road** 3 miles to **Comus**, then turn **right** on **Comus Road**. You will see **Sugarloaf Mountain** from here. Follow **Comus Road** straight into **Stronghold** to the entrance of the mountain. There is limited parking , so get here early!

☞   **From the Baltimore Beltway (695)** – Take **I-70 west** approximately 38 miles to **Frederick, MD**. From Frederick, follow **I-270 south** 9.5 miles to the **Hyattstown exit (Exit 22)**. Get on **Route 109 (Old Hundred Road)** and continue as above.

MILES   DIRECTIONS

0.0   **START** from the park entrance at the base of the mountain in Stronghold. Facing east, turn **left** on **SUGARLOAF MOUNTAIN ROAD**. This road starts out paved, then turns to gravel after a quarter-mile.

2.5   Turn **left** on **THURSTON ROAD** (paved).

4.8   Turn **hard left** on **PETERS ROAD** (becomes unpaved).

7.0   Turn **left** on **PARK MILLS ROAD** (paved).

7.7   Turn **left** on **MOUNT EPHRAIM ROAD** (unpaved).

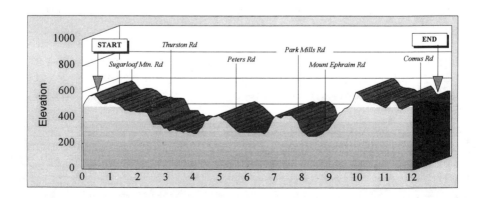

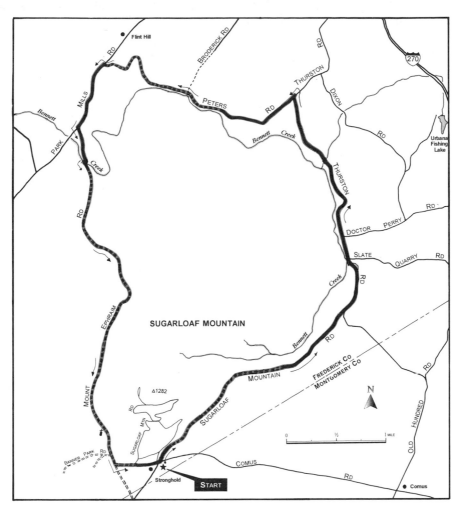

11.5 Turn **left** on **COMUS ROAD** (unpaved).

11.9 Arrive back at Stronghold. What a gorgeous ride!

(continued from page 91)

This is a great ride for cyclists wanting the adventure and unique scenery often associated with riding off the beaten path, but not interested in the severe challenges of singletrack trails twisting up and down the mountain slopes.

Ride Information

Trail Maintenance Hotline:

> *Stronghold Corporation*   *(301) 869-7846*
>
> *Sugarloaf Mountain Staff*   *(301) 874-2024*

Schedule:

> *Sugarloaf Mountain Park and Stronghold Corporation open daily from early morning to sunset, year-round*

Maps:

> *USGS maps:*   *Buckeystown, MD; Urbana, MD*
>
> *ADC maps:*   *Frederick road map*

Sugarloaf Mountain

10. Saddleback Trail

Start: *Sugarloaf park entrance*	**Terrain:** *Hilly singletrack, dirt roads*
Length: *7.7 miles*	**Riding Time:** *1 – 1½ hours*
Rating: *Moderate to difficult*	**Calories Burned:** *1000 – 1500*

Sugarloaf is a mountain well known to cyclists from all over the Washington, Baltimore, and Frederick area. This small mountain stands alone, nearly 800 feet above the surrounding Monocacy Valley, with a wonderful combination of forest roads and singletrack trails that wind back and forth beneath the thick woods covering its slopes.

Among Sugarloaf's network of trails and roads is the Saddleback Trail, a delight to hundreds of off-roaders, hikers, and equestrians who visit each year. Saddleback Trail, though, is a unique trail system, designed specifically to accomodate the growing number of mountain bikers and equestrians seeking solitude in the woods.

Built in 1993 under the supervision of the staff of the Stronghold Corporation, groups of off-road cyclists, hikers, and Boy Scouts worked together to create a trail that combines both forest roads and challenging singletrack. The result is a fantastic course ideal for mountain biking, hiking, and horseback riding.

The loop begins on the mountain's west face, following yellow blazes along a series of challenging singletrack. You can follow the yellow blazes along the entire ride without getting lost. The yellow

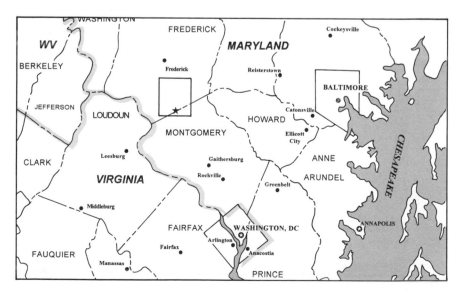

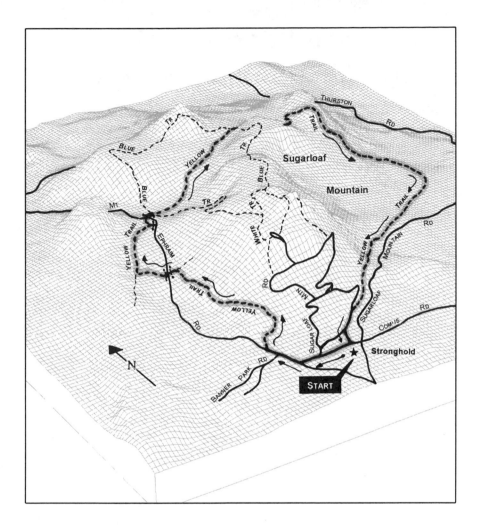

blazes lead you on Mount Ephraim Road for no more than one-tenth of a mile before you continue straight past a gate and start a steady, steep climb up the mountain to the east side. At the top of this climb, where the Blue, White, and Yellow Trails meet, is the "saddleback," for which this trail system is named. It's noticeable on the three-dimensional map as a dip between two of the mountain's lower peaks. Following the Yellow Trail, you will contour along the edge of the mountain around a small stream, suffer through one more quick but extreme uphill, then be rewarded with a fast and exhilarating half-mile descent down a forest road. This road eventually leads you back to a singletrack trail that rolls along the base of the mountain and returns to Stronghold.

(continued on page 101)

Saddleback Trail

☞   **From the Capital Beltway (495)** – Take **I-270 north** approximately 21 miles to the **Hyattstown exit (Exit 22)**. Circle under I-270, heading southwest on **Route 109 (Old Hundred Road)**. Follow **Old Hundred Road** 3 miles to **Comus**, then turn right on **Comus Road**. You will see **Sugarloaf Mountain** from here. Follow **Comus Road** straight into **Stronghold** to the entrance of the mountain. There is limited parking, so get here early.

☞   **From the Baltimore Beltway (695)** – Take **I-70 west** approximately 38 miles to **Frederick, MD**. From Frederick, follow **I-270 south** 9.5 miles to the **Hyattstown exit (Exit 22)**. Get on **Route 109 (Old Hundred Road)** and continue as above.

MILES   DIRECTIONS

0.0   **START** at the base of the mountain at the park entrance. Heading west, follow **COMUS ROAD** (becomes unpaved) toward **Mount Ephraim Road**.

0.3   At the stop sign, turn **right** on **MOUNT EPHRAIM ROAD.**

0.4   Turn **right** from Mount Ephraim Road into the woods on **SADDLEBACK TRAIL (Yellow Trail)**. This turn is no more than 50 feet past Banner Park Road. The trail is marked by three-inch **yellow-circle blazes**.

1.8   Saddleback Trail drops off on a gravel jeep trail. Turn **left,** riding toward Mount Ephraim Road.

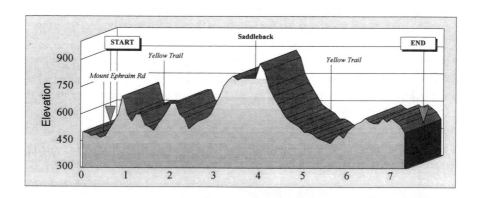

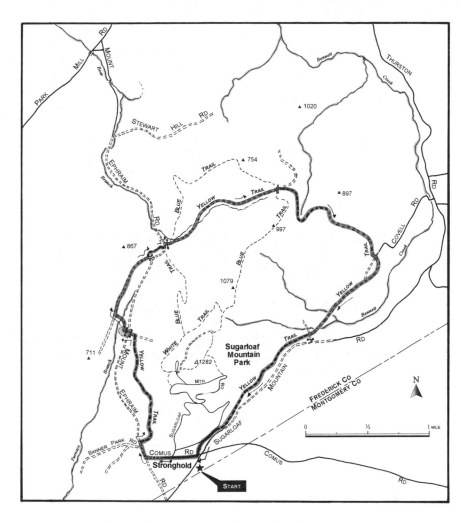

1.9 Cross **Mount Ephraim Road** through two gates and into a clearing. Stay to **right** through this clearing, passing the sign "Stewardship Demonstration Forest." Continue following the yellow blaze **SADDLEBACK TRAIL** down the hill, into the woods.

2.1 Stay **right** on **SADDLEBACK TRAIL**, following the yellow blaze.

2.8 Turn **left** on **MOUNT EPHRAIM ROAD**, continuing downhill. In just over one-tenth of a mile Mount Ephraim Road bears left. Go **straight** at this point through a small gate, beginning the long, steady climb up this jeep trail.

3.9   Reach the top of the climb. Go **straight** at this trail junction where the Blue Trail crosses the Yellow Trail.

This is the **saddleback**.

4.4   The trail contours along the mountain, horseshoing around a small stream. Bear **right**, following the yellow-blazed **SADDLEBACK TRAIL** up this short, steep climb.

4.6   Start the long descent down this forest road.

6.2   Reach the bottom of the descent. Turn **right**, just before a small house, on more singletrack. Continue following the yellow-blazed **SADDLEBACK TRAIL**.

6.4   Singletrack turns **right** on another jeep trail.

7.3   Saddleback trail empties out on Sugarloaf's **Entrance Road** (paved). Turn **left**, following this road downhill toward the main entrance.

7.7   Reach the park entrance in Stronghold.

Ride Information

Trail Maintenance Hotline:

Stronghold Corporation   *(301) 869-7846*

Sugarloaf Mountain Staff   *(301) 874-2024*

Schedule:

Open daily from early morning to sunset, year-round

Maps:

USGS maps: Buckeystown, MD; Urbana, MD
ADC maps: Frederick road map
Stronghold & Sugarloaf Mountain trail map

(continued from page 97)

Geologically speaking, Sugarloaf Mountain is what is called a monadnock. This is a hill or mountain that remains standing high above the surface after much of the surrounding land has eroded away. It took nearly 14 million years for Sugarloaf to look like it does today, and what a wonderful outdoor playground this process has created!

While you're riding, look for deer, raccoon, wild turkey, and even flying squirrels. But be especially careful because this is also home to the timber rattlesnake and the venomous copperhead!

11. Avalon

Start: *Rolling Rd Park & Ride*	Terrain: *Rugged singletrack*
Length: *8 miles*	Riding Time: *1½ – 2 hours*
Rating: *Difficult*	Calories Burned: *1500 – 2000*

Known simply as the Avalon Area by most cyclists, this small corner of Patapsco State Park is quite possibly one of Washington-Baltimore's most popular mountain biking playgrounds. Avalon's terrain is often severe and nearly always challenging, but for serious off-roaders, these conditions represent nothing less than prime mountain biking.

The ride begins at the Vineland trailhead (purple) on Rolling Road, and quickly takes you barreling downhill along twisting singletrack toward the river. At one point further along this trail you'll pass through a virtually pure beech forest which, in late autumn, resembles a tunnel of thick gold. Enjoy Grist Mill Trail (green) while you can, because this flat, paved path, that takes you over Patapsco's famous Swinging Bridge is but a brief respite before the challenges of the Orange Grove Area.

Like the beginning of the ride, the terrain through Orange Grove becomes quite severe. Much of the Blue Trail is quite steep and rocky. It is also the lcocation for off-road races held throughout the season. After negotiating the near vertical descent back to the river,

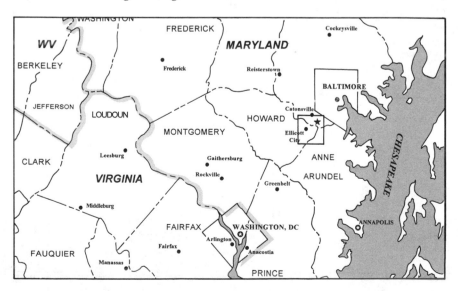

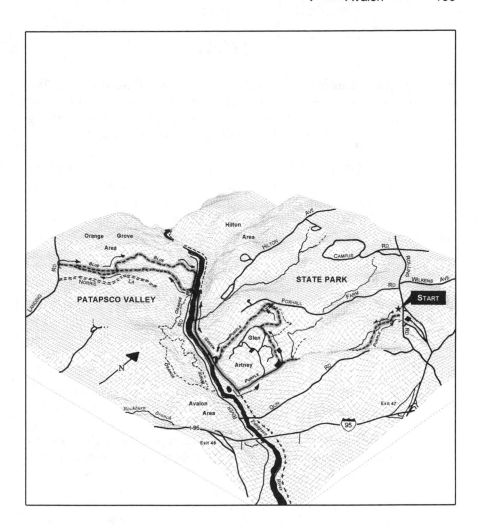

the ride returns, for the most part, along the same route. Before you head home make time to see one of Patapsco's most magnificent cascades just up the river from the Swinging Bridge.

It's worth noting that the course selected for this book is only one of a countless number of routes within the Avalon Area. At the time this book went to press, there was no significant challenge to mountain bike access on Patapsco's fantastic network of trails — all were open to riding. Along with Avalon's proximity to Baltimore, it's easy to understand why this ideal section of parkland is so popular among off-road cyclists. The area's popularity does, however, raise some concerns regarding overuse and trail damage. Hundreds of cyclists, hikers, and equestrians may crowd this trail system on any

(continued on page 108)

Avalon

☞   **From Baltimore** – Take **I-95 south** toward **Catonsville** to **Exit 47, Route 166 west**. Go west on **Route 166** four-tenths of a mile and stay in the **center lane**. This lane drops you directly into the **Parking Area**. Park here. The trail starts just across **Rolling Road**.

☞   **From Washington's Capital Beltway (495)** – Take **I-95 north** toward **Catonsville**, just south of Baltimore. Go on **I-95** 21 miles to **Exit 47, Route 166 west**. Go west on **Route 166** four-tenths of a mile and stay in the **center lane**. This lane drops you directly into the **Parking Area**. Park here. The trail starts just across **Rolling Road**.

MILES   DIRECTIONS

0.0   **START** at the **Park & Ride** parking lot in between the on-off ramps at Rolling Road. The trailhead starts on the other side of Rolling Road, no more than 50 feet to the left of the Park & Ride.

The trail begins just to the right of a small, steel gate. It heads straight into the woods, traveling first alongside a barbed-wire fence, then dropping down a steep, narrow descent. (The trail is marked with a **purple-circle blaze in a white square**. Follow this purple blaze all the way to the Patapsco River.)

0.5   Stay **right** at this little trail intersection.

1.0   Cross Soapstone Branch creek, then pedal straight through

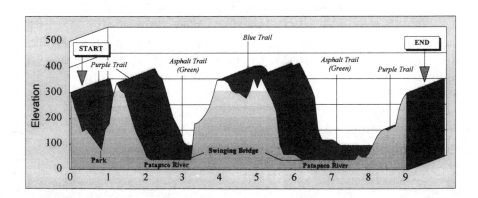

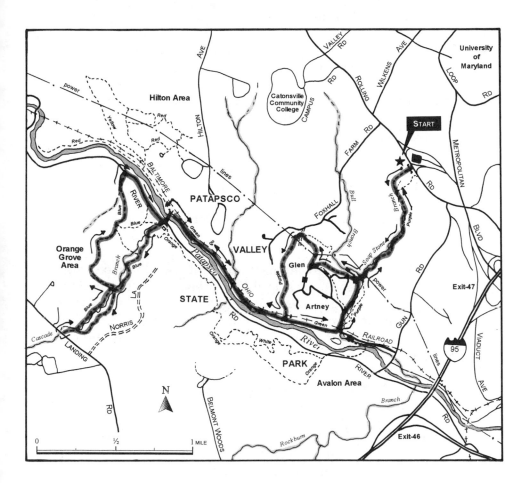

the parking lot at the **Glen Artney Area**. Pick up the **Purple Vineland Trail** straight across this parking area. The trail heads back into the woods and up a tough climb.

1.3 Turn **right** at the top of this climb on the paved park road. Continue uphill.

1.4 At the crest of this hill, just before the small parking area on the right, turn **right** off the paved road and pedal around an incomplete metal fence. The **Purple Trail** continues around the fence and up the hill.

1.5 Cross underneath the power lines. Begin a long, winding, technical descent.

1.7   Cross a dirt jeep trail.   Continue down the singletrack toward the river.

2.3   Reach the bottom of the descent. Ride through the stone tunnel to the bike path. Turn **right** on the **PAVED BIKE PATH** along the river.

3.4   Paved bike path ends. Turn **left** and cross the river over the **Swinging Bridge**.

A restroom and telephone is available on the other side of the river.

Once across the Swinging Bridge, you want to head **straight** into the woods, passing the bathrooms and telephone on your left, and ride the **BLUE TRAIL** up the steep climb along Cascade Branch creek into the Orange Grove Area. This climb, for anyone, should prove extremely difficult. Good luck!

The **Blue Trail** undulates along some very technical trails following the creek. Keep your eyes peeled for the Blue blazes.

4.0   The **Blue Trail** splits at this creek intersection. Stay **left**, heading toward Landing Road.

4.5   Reach **Landing Road**. Turn around and head back along the **BLUE TRAIL** on the opposite side of the creek.

4.9   Reach the trail intersection. Turn **left**, following the **BLUE TRAIL** away from the creek. This section of trail is very technical and ends with a nearly vertical descent down to the river.

5.7   Turn **right** on **RIVER ROAD**, then head east along the river.

6.1   Turn **left**, crossing the **Swinging Bridge** over the river. Turn **right** on the **paved bike path**.

Crossing Patapsco's Swinging Bridge

7.5 Reach the **Avalon Area**. Turn **left** under the **second tunnel** along the bike path. Follow the park road north along Soapstone Branch creek.

7.8 Turn **right** off the park road back into the woods on the **PURPLE VINELAND TRAIL**. You will have to cross the creek, then ride this rocky trail back up the hill to the Park & Ride.

8.8 Reach the top of this climb. Cross **Rolling Road** back to the **Park & Ride**. Talk about a brutal ride!

(continued from page 103)

given weekend, making trail maintenance a serious challenge. In order to maintain access to this priceless off-road habitat, make sure you get involved with local clubs, organizations, park officials, and other trail users to help preserve the trails and the integrity of the Avalon Area.

Ride Information

Trail Maintenance Hotline:

Patapsco Valley State Park HQ	*(410) 461-5005*
Emergency 24 hrs	*(410) 461-0050*
TTD	*(301) 974-3683*

Schedule:

Open from 10 A.M. to sunset, Thursday – Sunday

Maps:

USGS maps: Sykesville, MD
ADC maps: Carroll County, Baltimore County road maps
Patapsco Valley State Park trail map

12. Gambrill (Black Trail)

Start: *Trailhead parking lot*	**Terrain:** *Rocky singletrack*
Length: *2.7 miles*	**Riding Time:** *30 – 45 mins*
Rating: *Moderate to difficult*	**Calories Burned:** *500 – 1000*

Here's a small loop in Gambrill State Park that may be, for a cyclist new to singletrack, the best kind of introduction to white-knuckle trail riding. This route along the Black Trail will only take about half an hour to 45 minutes, which, for someone not yet ready for a long haul on terrain like this, should be plenty. The trail's terrain offers a mixture of fairly level sections with a few steep slopes to negotiate. Off-road cyclists eager for just a sampling of this high-speed, bone-jarring singletrack will love the moderate level of this trail, the exciting challenges it offers, the proximity to the car, and the breathtaking views of the valleys below.

You begin where all trails start in this park — at the parking lot on the east side of Gambrill Park Road, just before the steep climb to High Knob. The Black trail follows the same route as the Green, Red, and Yellow trails at first, then breaks off after about one-tenth of a mile and continues clockwise along the wooded slopes below High Knob. Much of this first section of trail is level, though rugged, and offers the opportunity to become familiar with riding along a narrow

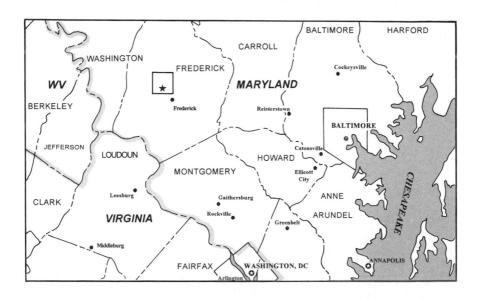

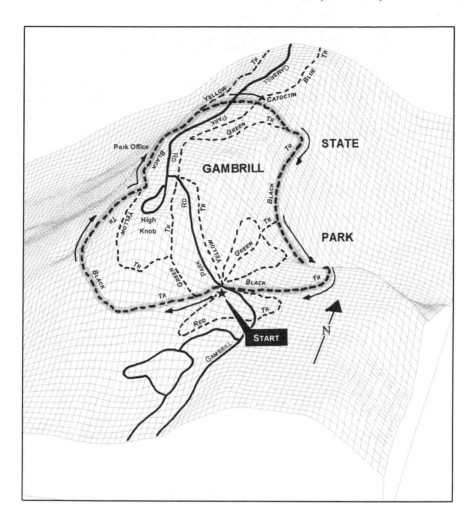

path. The terrain begins to change, however, as you continue around the west flank of the mountain where the trail narrows, then climbs toward the ridge line. Be sure to catch a view of the Middletown Valley along this section, but don't take your eyes off the trail for long or a tree root or rock may reach out and grab a wheel right out from under you!

As you cross Gambrill Park Road at the top of the mountain, detour right to the stone overlook facing out over Frederick Valley. The view is breathtaking! But it's time to get back to the trail, and for the new off-roader, your first real challenge awaits.

The Black Trail dives into the woods to the right of the main

(continued on page 114)

Gambrill (Black Trail)

☞   From Frederick, MD – Take **Route-40 west (Baltimore National Pike)** and turn **right** onto **Shookstown Road**. Follow **Shookstown Road** to **Gambrill Park Road** and turn **right**. Go 0.5 miles up **Gambrill Park Road** and park in the small parking lot on the **right** side of the road, just before the hill gets very steep at the top.

MILES   DIRECTIONS

0.0   **START** at the **TRAILHEAD** parking lot and follow the **BLACK TRAIL**, entering on the west side of the road and heading **south**. Follow the trail in a clockwise direction.

0.7   Reach the top of this first climb, near the main road. Turn **left** at the top, following the **BLACK TRAIL**.

0.9   Bear **right**, continuing up. Overlook on the left.

1.1   Yellow Trail and the Black Trail split. Follow the **BLACK TRAIL** to the **right**.

1.2   Cross **Gambrill Park Road**. The **BLACK TRAIL** continues across the road to the left. There is a stone overlook to the right of this point, across the road.

1.3   The **BLACK TRAIL** splits to the **right,** continuing downhill. The Yellow Trail goes to the left. This is a very steep descent.

1.4   The **Black Trail** drops straight off to the **Catoctin (Blue**

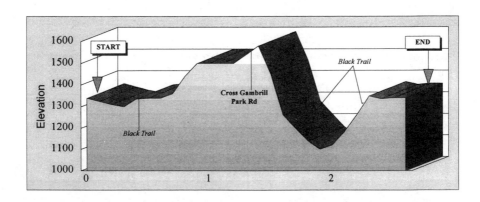

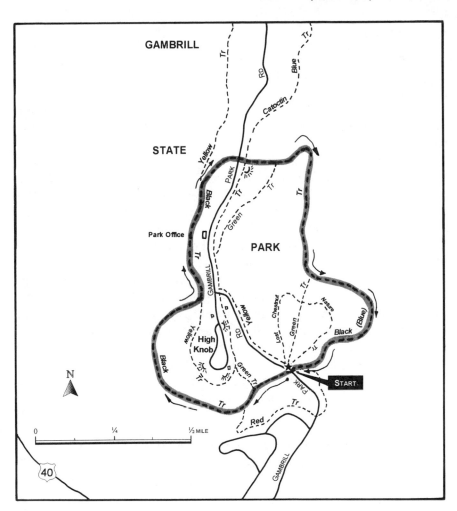

Trail). Turn **left** on this dirt road, following the combined **BLACK/BLUE TRAIL**.

1.5   Turn **right** at this intersection, following the **BLACK TRAIL** marker next to the painted tree.

2.1   Turn **left**, following the **BLACK TRAIL** marker. Begin final steep climb back to the parking lot.

2.7   Reach the parking lot. Whew!

(continued from page 111)

road and follows the yellow and black blazes down a short, steep, rocky trail. You get a small break along a shallow descent on a wide forest road, but this soon ends, and you must bear left off the road and follow the black and blue blazes. Black and blue may prove appropriate when you reach the bottom of this steep and challenging rocky descent.

In the sport of off-road cycling, descending steep, narrow singletrack trails is often more physically demanding than pedaling uphill on smooth surfaces. These bone-jarring descents require the strength of your whole body to direct the bike correctly over rocks, stumps, roots, and crevices. You must remain intensely focused on the trail to counter all obstacles that will get in your way. Through all this, you must also ride smoothly to absorb the shock pounding through your arms and legs. Downhills in trail riding are not often places for resting, and this trail is no exception. New riders will be treated to their first world-class, bone-jarring descent down this trail, and veterans of the sport will have their hands full as well.

The ride is not over, though. Just when this wild descent comes to an end, a long, rocky climb back to the parking lot begins. Take this climb slowly and enjoy your surroundings. In May and early June you will be treated to an abundance of blooming dogwood trees

Ride Information

Trail Maintenance Hotline:

> South Mountain Recreation Area   (301) 791-4767
>
> TDD   (301) 974-3683

Cost:

> Only for use of the picnic shelters, Tea Room, and campsites

Schedule:

> Open daily from dawn to sunset

Maps:

> USGS maps: Myersville, MD; Catoctin Furnace, MD
>
> Middletown, MD; Frederick, MD
>
> ADC maps: Frederick, MD road map
>
> Gambrill State Park trail map

and the beautiful pink flowers of the mountain laurel. For those on their first trip off the road and into the woods, you should enjoy this magnificent ride as you travel the trails in the incomparable Catoctin Forest.

Fletcher Harris

13. Catoctin Blue Trail

Start: *Gambrill State Park*	**Terrain:** *Rugged singletrack, roads*
Length: *10.5*	**Riding Time:** *1½ – 2 hours*
Rating: *Very difficult*	**Calories Burned:** *1500 – 2000*

The terrain is steep, the rocks are hard, and the trail is mostly unforgivable. This is perhaps one of Maryland's toughest trails open to mountain bike riding.

The Catoctin Trail leads you deep into Gambrill and Frederick State Forest over relentless singletrack that will have your body aching for pavement — that is unless you've loaded the suspension onto your bike. For those skeptics of bicycle suspension, here's your chance to test its metal.

On the lighter side, tall stands of chestnut oak, hickory, and black birch canopy the Catoctin Mountain, shielding out hints of a more hectic world beyond its wooded boundaries. Only refreshing sounds of cascading streams, calling birds, and the footsteps of local deer are heard — and the occasional sound of bicycle chains slapping against frames as cyclists warily negotiate their way down the rugged trails.

The Catoctin Trail starts where all trails begin in Gambrill — from the parking lot on the east side of Gambrill Park Road. In its entirety, the Catoctin Trail travels north nearly 18 miles through

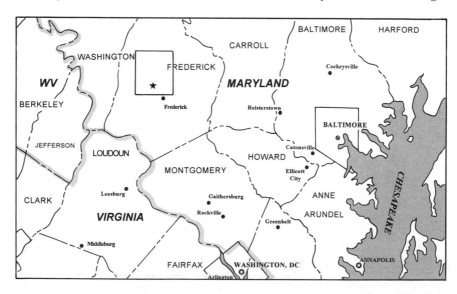

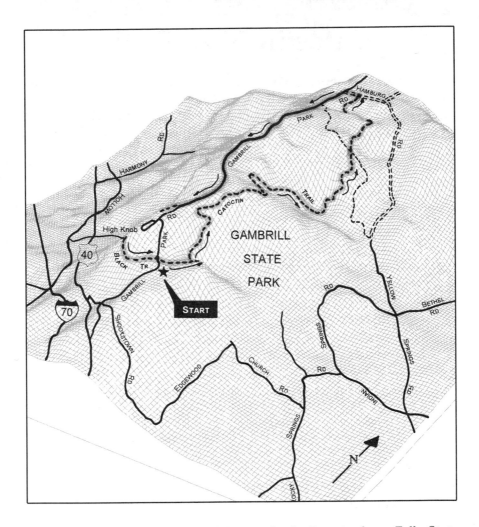

Gambrill State Park, Frederick Watershed, Cunningham Falls State Park, and Catoctin Mountain National Park. Unfortunately, mountain bike access is cut short just north of Frederick Watershed. Follow the dark blue blazes up and down Catoctin's steep, jagged slopes all the way to Hamburg Road.

The name "Catoctin" is believed to come from a tribe of Native Americans called Kittoctons, living at the foothills of the mountains along the Potomac. European settlers first arrived in 1732 from Philadelphia, attracted by Lord Baltimore's offer of 200 acres of rent-free land for three years. The land would then cost only one cent per acre per year. Much of the land used by these early settlers was for logging and for supplying charcoal to local iron furnaces. Catoctin's

(continued on page 121)

Catoctin Blue Trail

☞   From Frederick, MD – Take **Route 40 west (Baltimore National Pike)** and turn **right** on **Shookstown Road**.   Follow **Shookstown Road** to **Gambrill Park Road** and turn **right**.   Go 0.5 miles up **Gambrill Park Road** and park in the small parking lot on the **right** side of the road, just before the road gets very steep.

MILES   DIRECTIONS

0.0   **START** at the **TRAILHEAD** parking lot and follow the **BLUE TRAIL** into the forest, heading north. This quickly becomes a steep, rocky, fast descent straight down the mountain.

0.6   Come to a trail intersection. Turn **right**, following the **BLUE TRAIL** (indicated by the blue blazes on the trees).

0.7   Bear **left** up the mountain, continuing on the **BLUE/ YELLOW TRAIL**.

1.4   Reach the summit of this brutally steep climb. **Blue/Yellow Trail** splits. Turn **left** off the present trail, then immediately **right**, continuing on the **BLUE TRAIL**. The **Yellow Trail** goes left at this point and heads back toward High Knob.

1.6   Turn **right** on the **DIRT ROAD**. (You will turn off this road very soon.)

1.65   Turn **left** off the dirt road back into the woods, continuing

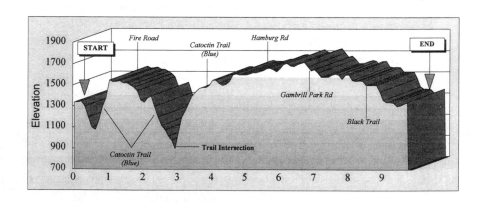

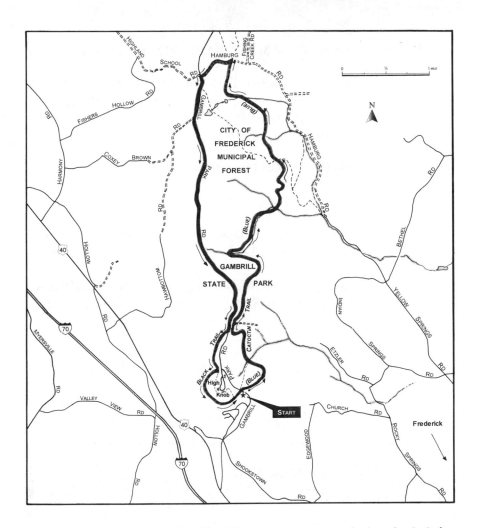

on the **BLUE TRAIL**. (Keep your eyes peeled to the **left** for the blue blazes on the trees. This trailhead is difficult to spot.) Begin a very long, steep, rocky descent down the mountain.

2.8   Reach the bottom of the long, rocky descent. The forest here is breathtaking. Turn **left**, crossing the stream, and continue on the **BLUE TRAIL**. Start climbing again up the mountain. This climb is even more brutal than the last!

3.6   Reach the summit. Finally! How does your back feel?

5.5   Turn **left** on **HAMBURG ROAD** (unpaved).

5.9   Turn **left** on **GAMBRILL PARK ROAD** (paved).

9.3   Turn **right** off **Gambrill Park Road** to the **BLACK TRAIL**. This turn-off is just before the first **stone overlook** on the left side of Gambrill Park Road. (You should see the **Black arrow** pointing the way.)

9.4   Turn **left** on the **YELLOW/BLACK TRAIL**.

9.6   Bear **left**, continuing down. Overlook on the right.

9.8   Turn **right** at the turn near the main road, continuing to follow the **BLACK TRAIL**.

10.5   Cross Gambrill Park Road and arrive at the **TRAILHEAD** parking lot. You deserve a serious drink after that ride!

Ride Information

Trail Maintenance Hotline:

South Mountain Recreation Area	*(301) 791-4767*
TDD	*(301) 974-3683*

Cost:

Only to use the picnic shelters, Tea Room, and campsites

Schedule:

Open daily from dawn to sunset

Maps:

USGS maps: *Myersville, MD; Catoctin Furnace, MD*
                        Middletown, MD; Frederick, MD
ADC maps: *Frederick, MD road map*
Gambrill State Park trail map

(continued from page 117)

resources, though, were eventually stripped and depleted from extensive clear-cutting.   Then, in 1935, the federal government purchased more than 10,000 acres of this land to be made into a recreational area.   The National Park Service and Maryland Park Service manage the land today, permitting Catoctin to redevelop back into the hardwood forest of pre-European settlement.

This trail is **not** recommended to the novice off-road cyclist, and should be considered extremely challenging to those well-versed in rugged terrain.

14. Accotink Trail

Start: *Wakefield Park*	**Terrain:** *Singletrack/dirt trails*
Length: *6.1 miles*	**Riding Time:** *1 hour*
Rating: *Easy*	**Calories Burned:** *600 – 1000*

Sometimes it's interesting to see where you find singletrack. Typically, the great trails lie west or far north of the Washington suburbs. Out there, usually a "long drive" from where most of us live, singletrack and forest roads trace the landscape in all directions. The dirt's the limit. "If only we lived closer to the trails," goes the suburban cyclist's woeful anthem.

But a closer look reveals we *do* live near the trails, thanks to the Fairfax County Park Authority. Wakefield and Lake Accotink Parks, less than half a mile from the Capital Beltway in Fairfax County, are filled with a network of fun, technical singletrack. Most of these singletrack trails are offshoots from the park's main loop, which is a scenic, wooded dirt trail around Accotink's beautiful 70-acre lake.

The Accotink Trail itself was once part of Orange and Alexandria Railroad's original roadbed built in the early 1850s. The rails and ties, of course, have since been removed, and a new rail was laid farther south along a straighter route. Lake Accotink's history began in the 1930s when the U.S. Army Corps of Engineers dammed Accotink Creek to create a reservoir for Fort Belvoir, nearly five miles

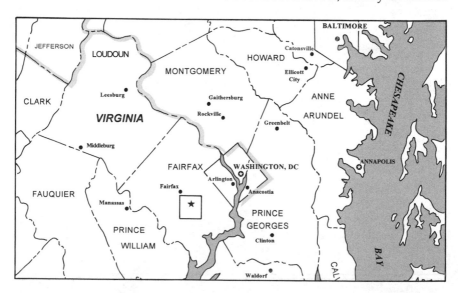

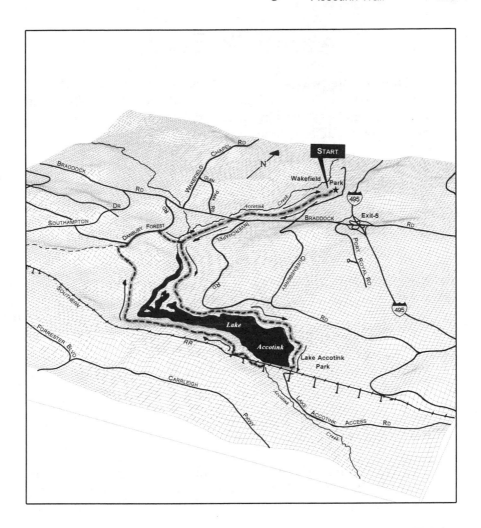

downstream. The lake and surrounding land was given to Fairfax County in 1965 by the federal government for park and recreational use. The park's great trails, open to bicycling, have been "maturing" ever since.

This ride begins from Wakefield Park and travels south along the Accotink Trail around the lake, then back to Wakefield. There are even some great trails that go north from Wakefield and cross challenging routes beneath the power lines.

For thrill seekers, there is an abundance of short, steep hills, tree roots, quick dips, and fast turns. For the off-road cyclist with a lighter touch, Accotink Trail takes you through a scenic woodland preserve, quiet and relaxing in the spring and summer, breathtaking

(continued on page 127)

Accotink Trail

☞   **From the Beltway (495)** – Exit **West** on **Braddock Road (Exit 5)**. In less than 0.2 miles, turn **right** onto Wakefield Park's **Entrance Road**. Go 0.6 miles to parking and recreation center on the left. Telephones, water, toilets, food, etc.

MILES   DIRECTIONS

0.0   **START** at **Wakefield Park Recreation Center** near the big green recycling bins. The trail begins up near the park entrance road and heads south through Wakefield toward Braddock Road.

0.2   Cross the athletic fields parking lot. **ACCOTINK TRAIL** continues on the other side of parking lot.

0.6   Cross under **Braddock Road**.

0.7   Just across Braddock Road, **bear left**, continuing on the main trail.

1.0   Stay **left** at the fork in the trail, following the wooden **ACCOTINK TRAIL** post.

2.1   Trail comes to a T. **Turn right**, following **ACCOTINK TRAIL**. The creek should be on your right. This part of the trail winds up and down through the woods — a lot of fun.

2.9   Arrive at **Lake Accotink's marina**.

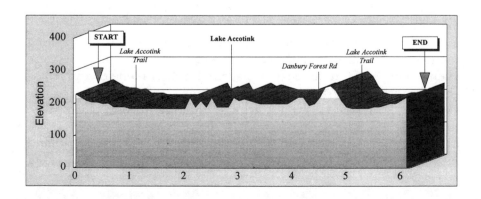

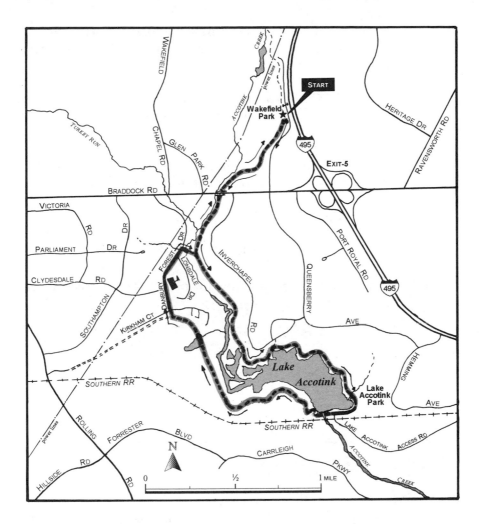

Concessions, food, drinks, putt-putt golf, canoe and boat rental, etc.

Stay **right**, crossing the parking lot toward the dam.

3.0 Cross **Lake Accotink Dam**. Follow the bike path parallel to the train trestle and head toward the woods.

3.3 Reenter the woods on the dirt bike trail. (Steep hill to this dirt path.)

4.5 Turn **hard-right** off the dirt path onto the asphalt trail, taking you down onto **DANBURY FOREST DRIVE** in the neighborhood of Danbury Forest. **Kings Glen Elementary School** on the right.

4.9   Reenter **ACCOTINK TRAIL** on the right just after **Lonsdale Drive.** This is a steep descent alongside the concrete steps into the woods.

5.0   Turn **right** off the asphalt path, following **ACCOTINK TRAIL** across a wooden foot bridge over Accotink creek.

5.1   Turn **left** onto **ACCOTINK TRAIL**.

5.5   Cross under **Braddock Road**.

6.1   Arrive back at the parking lot of **Wakefield Recreation Center**.

Ride Information

Trail Maintenance Hotline:

    Fairfax County Park Authority   *(703) 246-5700*

    Lake Accotink   *(703) 569-3464*

Schedule:

    Open daylight to dark all year-round

Maps:

    USGS maps: *Annandale, VA*

    ADC map: *Northern Virginia road map*

    Fairfax County Park Authority trail map

(continued from page 123)

in the fall. Who says you have to drive far to get out of the gridlock and into the woods? For Beltway commuters, Accotink is less than a stone's throw away.

Going down to Accotink Dam

15. Burke Lake Loop

Start: *South Run Park*	**Terrain:** *Flat, asphalt, dirt trails*
Length: *7.3 miles*	**Riding Time:** *1 hour*
Rating: *Easy*	**Calories Burned:** *600 – 1000*

This spring the government chose Burke for the new airport. The whole town was shocked. 4,500 acres has been condemned. The town hasn't been the same since. Over 100 families are forced to find new homes by May 1, 1952.

Virginia Lee Fowler
October 11, 1951

This was the mood of the people of Burke, who were told in the early 1950s that the U.S. government planned to build a huge space-age airport in the town of Burke, Virginia. Had it not been for some great leaders in the town's fight against this proposal, what is now Dulles Airport would have been built on the exact parcel of land you see on this map. Having lost the battle, the U.S. government reconsidered its original plan and decided instead on a large tract of undeveloped land in Chantilly. As we know, Dulles Airport is one of the nation's largest international ports, with regularly scheduled flights by the awesome 747 passenger jets and the supersonic Concord

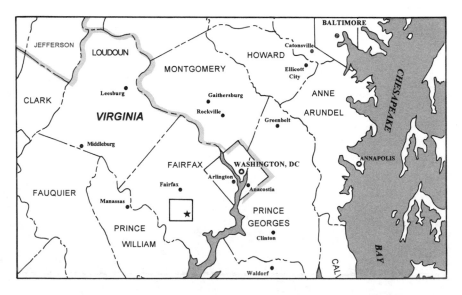

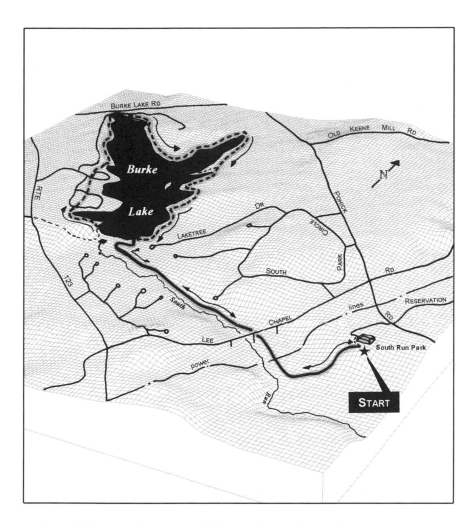

— how different things would have been. Instead, the government publicly auctioned the parcels of land set aside for the original Burke Airport site on Saturday, June 13, 1959. Nearly 900 acres were given to the Fairfax County Park Authority, who, in the 1960s, dammed streams and flooded 218 acres to create Burke Lake.

This ride begins behind the field house at South Run Park and follows South Run north to Burke Lake. Unique and colorful gardens grow along the South Run trail, tilled by the residents of South Park Circle.

Surrounded by wooded parkland, it's easy to agree that Burke Lake, Fairfax County's largest lake, is also one of the region's prettiest, most peaceful places for a bike ride. The gravel and dirt trail

(continued on page 133)

Burke Lake Loop

☞   **From the Beltway (495)** – take **I-95 south** toward Richmond. Go only about 0.5 miles to the Springfield **Exit 57, Route 644 west (Old Keene Mill Road)**. Follow **Old Keene Mill Road** west 4 miles, then turn **left** on **Huntsman Boulevard**. Follow Huntsman Boulevard 1.5 miles to Pohick Road. Turn **right** on **Pohick Road**, go about 0.3 miles, and turn **left** into **South Run District Park**. Parking, water, telephones, toilets, showers.

MILES   DIRECTIONS

0.0   **START** at **South Run Park** behind South Run Recreation Center (main building at park). Follow the **paved path** from the rear parking area down the hill into the woods.

0.2   Reach the bottom of the hill and follow the **asphalt BIKE PATH** along **South Run**. The stream should be on your left.

0.4   Cross underneath the power lines.

0.6   Cross underneath Lee Chapel Road.

1.5   Arrive at **Burke Lake** and turn **left**, crossing the **dam**.

1.7   Reach the other side of the dam. Continue along the gravel **BICYCLE & WALKING PATH**, following the **Park Trail** signs.

2.0   Reach a small parking lot and boat ramp at the end of the

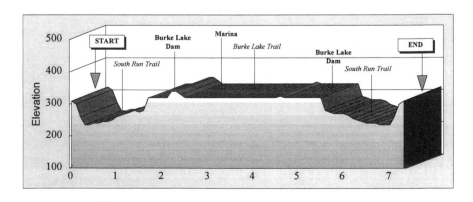

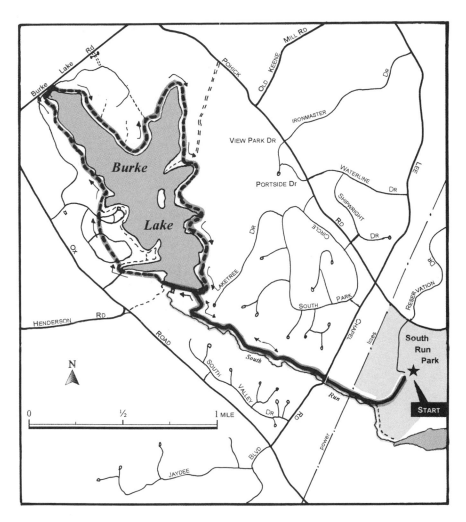

cove. Follow the **Park Trail** signs.

2.2   Cross a small open field. Stay to the **right side** of the field. The trail picks up on the other side. (Trail markings are obscure here, so keep a sharp eye.)

2.4   Cross the park road leading to Burke Lake Park's Marina. Follow the **Park Trail** signs across the road back into the woods.

Concession stand with food and drinks, boat rentals, bathrooms, etc., at the marina.

Stay **left** on the trail, going around the **frisbee golf course.**

3.3   The trail drops out onto the paved park road. Turn **right** on this road, cross the bridge, then reenter the trail back into the woods. (Burke Lake Road is on your left.) Continue following the trail around the lake.

6.0   Reach the **dam**. The loop around Burke Lake is complete. Stay to the **left** and follow the **asphalt BICYCLE PATH** along **South Run** back to South Run Park.

7.1   Cross underneath the power lines.

7.3   Bear **left** up the asphalt path to **South Run Park**.

7.5   Reach South Run Park's **Recreation Center.**

Ride Information

Trail Maintenance Hotline:

    Fairfax County Park Authority   *(703) 246-5700*

    Burke Lake Park   *(703) 323-6600*

Costs:

    $3.50 per car for nonresidents of Fairfax County at Burke Lake

Schedule:

    Open daily from dawn until dusk, mid-March to mid-November
    Trail is open year-round

Maps:

    USGS maps: *Fairfax, VA; Occoquan, VA*
    ADC map: *Northern VA road map*
    Burke Lake Park trail map

(continued from page 129)

around the lake is flat, meandering along the shoreline. From this trail, you can view hundreds of birds as they come and go to their temporary home during the spring and fall migrations.

This ride does not have to start at South Run Park, of course, and can easily be altered to begin at Burke Lake. But be prepared for a $3.50 fee charged per car to nonresidents of Fairfax County.

Everyone enjoys Burke Lake

16. Great Falls

Start: *Visitors Center*	**Terrain:** *Rocky, dirt trails; fire roads*
Length: *6.8 miles*	**Riding Time:** *1 – 1½ hours*
Rating: *Moderate*	**Calories Burned:** *800 – 1500*

At this spectacular national park, one of the most popular in the United States and located just 14 miles from our nation's capital, mountain bikers not only are allowed, but are welcome.

Along with hikers, rock climbers, historians, and kayakers, off-road cyclists come in droves to enjoy Great Falls' public resources. There are over five miles of designated trails to enjoy in this park, all of which can be mixed together to create hours of off-road adventure. The trails vary in intensity, ranging from rolling forest roads beneath tall oaks and maples to steep and rocky singletrack along the park's ridge line, overlooking the dramatic Mather Gorge. Because of the park's unequaled beauty, its proximity to Washington, and trail access to mountain bikes, it's no wonder Great Falls is Northern Virginia's most popular off-road cycling haven.

The ride begins at the visitors center parking lot and travels south along Old Carriage Road through the middle of the park. Old Carriage once carried settlers in the 1700s to their dwellings at Matildaville, ruins of which still stand today. This small town was developed by Henry Lee, a Revolutionary War hero and friend of

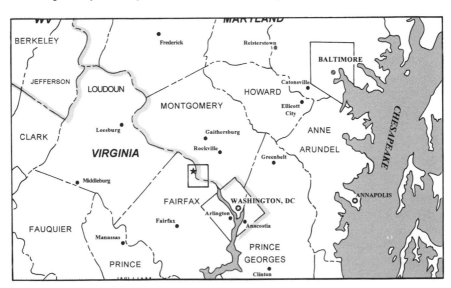

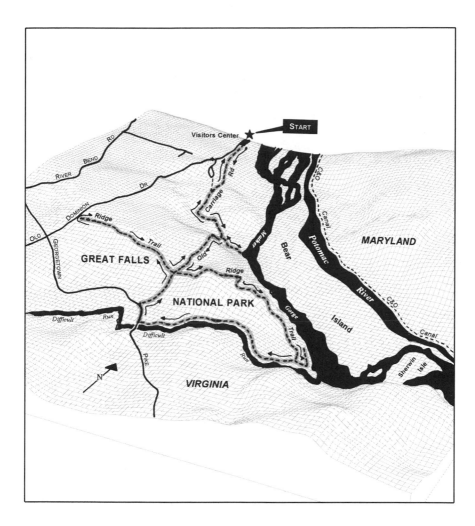

George Washington. Named after Lee's first wife, Matildaville lasted only three decades before fading into history.

The route turns after reaching deep into the park and travels up and down the rocky pass along Ridge Trail. During the winter months, breathtaking views of the gorge show through the trees. The trail then descends quickly to the Potomac *(another great view)* and follows along Difficult Run before heading north again back toward the start.

Great Falls has always been a popular place to visit for local and world tourists alike. Some have come to survey the river's rapids, such as George Washington, who, in 1784, formed the Patowmack Company to build a series of canals around the falls. Theodore

(continued on page 139)

Great Falls

☞   **From the Beltway (495)** – From **Exit-13** northwest of McLean, take **Route 193 (Georgetown Pike) west** toward **Great Falls**. Go about 4 miles, then turn **right** on **Old Dominion Drive**. Go 1 mile to the end of the **park entrance road,** and park at the **visitors center**. Telephones, water, food, toilet, information.

MILES   DIRECTIONS

0.0   **START** at **Great Falls Visitors Center**. Follow the **Horse/ Biker trail** south along **Entrance Road**.

0.4   Bear **right** at the restrooms and go around the steel gate on **OLD CARRIAGE ROAD** (unpaved).

1.1   Bear **left** down this trail to **Sandy Landing**.

1.3   Arrive at **Sandy Landing**. A beautiful spot along the river, great for viewing Mather Gorge. Return to **Old Carriage Road**.

1.5   Turn **left**, continuing on **OLD CARRIAGE ROAD**. Begin a steady uphill.

1.9   Turn **left** near the top of this climb on **RIDGE TRAIL**.

2.7   After the steep descent, turn **left** on **DIFFICULT RUN TRAIL**, heading toward the Potomac.

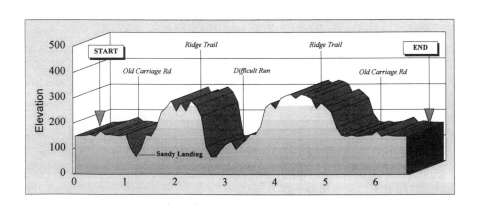

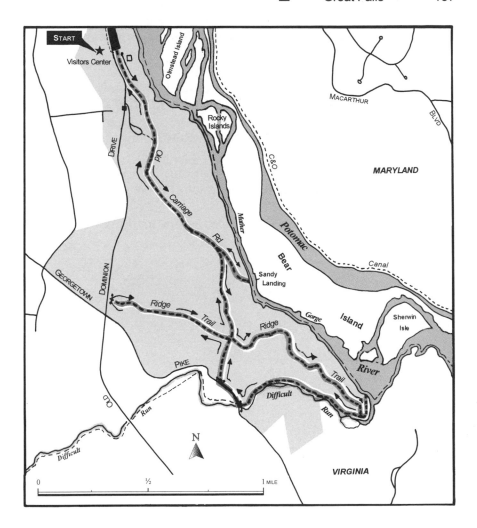

2.9 Arrive at the **Potomac River**. This is another great spot to view Sherwin Island, where Mather Gorge and the Potomac River converge. Turn around and follow **DIFFICULT RUN TRAIL** west along Difficult Run Creek toward Georgetown Pike.

3.6 Turn **right** on **GEORGETOWN PIKE**. Be careful with traffic, and ride on the dirt shoulder.

3.8 Turn **right** on **OLD CARRIAGE ROAD**. This is the first dirt road you come to on Georgetown Pike. Go around the gate and begin climbing.

4.0   Turn **left** on **RIDGE TRAIL**. Follow this toward the entrance road.

4.7   Reach Great Falls' entrance road (Old Dominion Road). **Turn around** and continue back on **RIDGE TRAIL**.

5.4   Turn **left** on **OLD CARRIAGE ROAD**.

6.4   Go through the gate at the beginning of Old Carriage Road, and head back to the parking lot at the visitors center.

6.8   Arrive back at the **visitors center** and parking lot.

Ride Information

Trail Maintenance Hotline:

National Park Service   *(703) 759-2915*

Costs:

$2.00 entrance fee is charged

Schedule:

Park is open from 7:00 A.M. to sunset, closed after dark

Maps:

USGS maps: Vienna, VA; Falls Church, VA
ADC maps: Northern Virginia road map
National Park Service Official trail map and guide

(continued from page 135)

Roosevelt came to Great Falls to hike and ride when he was president, calling it "the most beautiful place around here." And today, some of the most notable folks in the region come to enjoy Great Falls as well. But these folks don't come to build canals, develop towns, make trade, or seek solitude from the presidential office. We noteworthy folks come only to ride the great trails and carry on the heritage of our fat-tired sport.

Taking a break along Difficult Run

17. Prince William Forest Park

Start: *Visitors Center*	**Terrain:** *Hilly forest roads*
Length: *8+ miles of dirt roads*	**Riding Time:** *Varies with each ride*
Rating: *Moderate*	**Calories Burned:** *Varies w/ea. ride*

At one time Prince William's thousands of acres of forest land was extensively farmed for tobacco. Then when the hills eroded and the earth could no longer support their crops, farmers turned to dairy farming, already well established throughout the county. But this too failed for those living in the Quantico Creek area. The Civil War was equally taxing for those already struggling here. The Confederates blockaded the Potomac, requiring large numbers of troops for support. Those living in the vicinity of the blockade were required to provide the troops with timber and food and found that what little they had before the war was no longer enough.

A mining operation near the confluence of the north and south branches of Quantico Creek provided a much-needed boost to the area's economy in 1889. But a strike over wages closed the high-grade pyrite ore mine in 1920, bringing down with it any hope for the area's recovery. It was soon thereafter that the United States Government bought the land, resettling nearly 150 families, and with the Civilian Conservation Corps began the effort to "return the depleted land to an ecological balance."

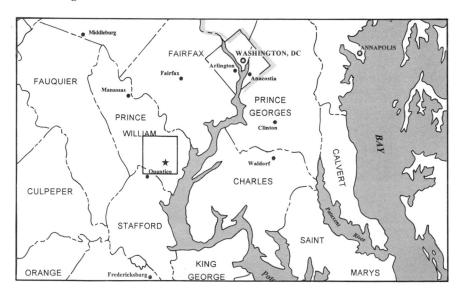

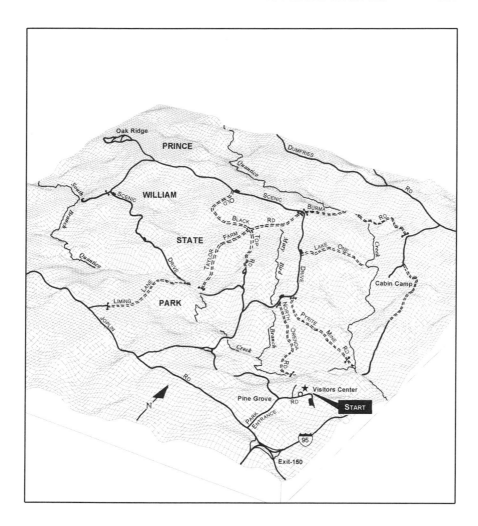

Prince William Forest Park now offers all kinds of outdoor activities for haggled Washingtonians to enjoy, one of which is bicycling. Riding on park trails, unfortunately, is prohibited. However, there are many unpaved, dirt roads throughout the park that *can* be used by cyclists. Many of these roads are separate out-and-back fire roads, in which case you may need to ride along paved Scenic Drive Road to create loops. Scenic Drive Road is very well maintained and even has its own bike lane.

To witness the absolute progress the forest has made in reclaiming what was once depleted and eroding farmland is a wonderful experience when you visit this 18,000-acre forest. And riding your mountain bike along the forest roads through the park gives you an up-close look at this process in action.

Prince William Forest Park

☞   From the Capital Beltway (495) – Take I-95 south toward Richmond for 20 miles to Exit 150, VA Route 619 west (Joplin Road). Turn right from Joplin Road in one-tenth of a mile to the Park Entrance Road. The visitors center is about one mile down this road. Telephone, bathroom, park information and trail maps here.

— NOTE —

All of these trails connect with Scenic Drive Road (paved). Leave your car at the visitors center, and ride to the start of each trail, or park along Scenic Drive Road near each trailhead and start from there. Parking lots along Scenic Drive Road are shown on the road map as small black squares.

TRAIL DESCRIPTIONS

Old Black Top Road

1.6 miles long. Old Black Top Road starts from the Turkey Run Parking area and travels north, crosses Taylor Farm Road, then connects with Scenic Drive Road. The terrain is moderate and offers a good challenge through the middle of the park.

Burma Road

1.5 miles long. Burma Road starts out as an easy forest road, then crosses over a series of hills, making this section moderately difficult. This forest road crosses Quantico Creek and takes you to Pleasant Road. From here, you have the possibility to create a loop back to Scenic Drive Road. Following Pleasant Road past Cabin Camp you can gather "fool's gold" at the site of the old pyrite mine. Cross Quantico Creek again and take Pyrite Mine Road back to Scenic Drive

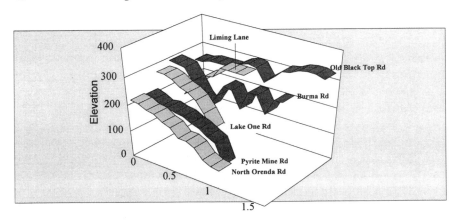

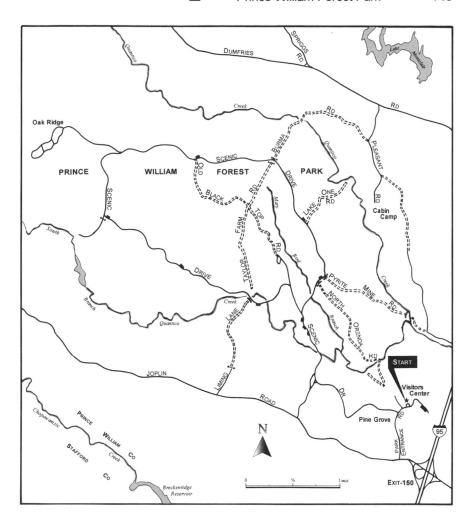

Road.

Taylor Farm Road

1.5 miles long. From the northern part of Scenic Drive Road, Taylor Farm Road is mostly level until it drops sharply to the South Branch Quantico Creek. The first nine-tenths of this road are part of the 9.7-mile South Valley Trail, which travels the circumference of this section of Prince William Forest Park.

North Orenda Road

1.2 miles long. This is a moderate forest road that takes you down to the South Branch. Across the creek is South Orenda Fire Road, leading you back to the visitors center.

Pyrite Mine Road

1.0 miles long. This forest road takes you from Scenic Drive Road to Quantico Creek, the North Valley Trail, and the old pyrite mine. The trail is moderate in the beginning, then becomes steep at the end.

Liming Lane Fire Road

0.8 miles long. This forest road is, for the most part, moderately easy. It begins from the parking lot on Scenic Drive Road and takes you out of the park's boundaries to Joplin Road.

Lake One Road

0.6 miles long. Lake One Road starts from the parking lot along Scenic Drive Road and takes you down a moderately steep hill to Quantico Creek.

Ride Information

Trail Maintenance Hotline:

Prince William Forest Park visitors center   *(703) 221-7181*

National Park Service   *(703) 759-2915*

Costs:

$3.00 per vehicle within the park

Schedule:

Visitors Center open between 8:30 A.M. and 5:00 P.M.

Maps:

USGS maps: Joplin, VA; Quantico, VA, MD
ADC maps: Prince William County road map
Prince William Forest Park trail map

Fletcher Harris

18. Middleburg Vineyard Tour

Start: *Middleburg Elem. School*	**Terrain:** *Rolling unpaved roads*
Length: *23.1 miles*	**Riding Time:** *2 –2½ hours*
Rating: *Moderate to difficult*	**Calories Burned:** *1500 – 2000*

Ah, wine! To sip the fruit is lots of fun, but to ride and drink can't be outdone.

Yes, this ride travels through some of Virginia's finest wine country, where visits to the vineyards are always welcome and wine tasting is just part of the tour.

You start in the historic town of Middleburg, a small, touristy outpost in the middle of Hunt Country. Horses abound in this magnificent countryside. A town with a rich history, Middleburg has enjoyed its share of good fortune. Established in 1787, this centuries-old town was even graced by a U.S. president when the Kennedy family attended the local Catholic church and built a home just outside town.

The ride starts on a route toward Piedmont Vineyard but breaks off from the main road onto backcountry dirt, perfect for an off-road tourist. This first section rolls comfortably past small estates and low-key horse farms. But when you turn east, the roads lift you into the hills. You'll pass some of the old and new — abandoned stone

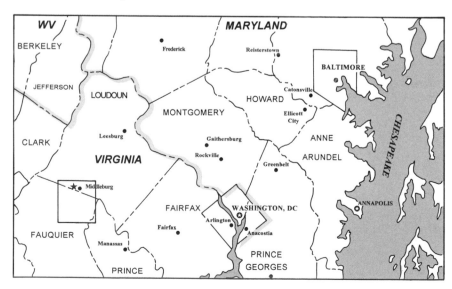

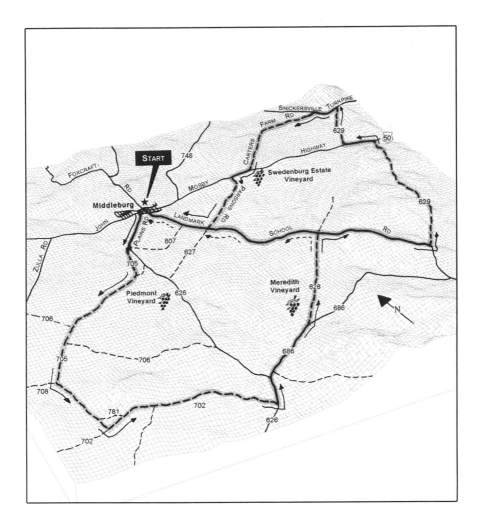

houses and modern, state-of-the-art homes — then head toward Meredith Vineyard to lavish in the land of the well-to-do. Gorgeous estates rest on acres of open land, where thoroughbreds graze in the warm sun. What a wonderful place to ride and dream. But don't forget to stop at the winery. The rest of the ride rolls up and down below Bull Run Mountain, taking you past one more vineyard, the Swedenburg Estate, before leading you back into Middleburg.

If the wine doesn't get the best of you, then enjoy the endless dirt roads scattered throughout this region. This is excellent off-road riding for cyclists looking for a change.

Middleburg Vineyard Tour

☞   **From the Capital Beltway (495)** – Take **I-66 west** 8.5 miles to **Exit 57, Route 50 west.** Go 23 miles on **Route 50 west** into **Middleburg.** John Mosby Highway (Route 50) becomes **Washington Street** within Middleburg town limits. From Washington Street, turn **right** on **Route 626, Madison Street.** Go 0.1 miles and turn **right** into the **Middleburg Elementary School** parking lot.

MILES   DIRECTIONS

0.0   **START** at the Middleburg Elementary School parking lot. Turn **left** on **ROUTE 626, MADISON STREET** (paved).

0.1   Turn **right** on **WASHINGTON STREET (ROUTE 50)** (paved).

0.3   Turn **left** on **PLAINS ROAD (ROUTE 626).** Follow the purple vineyard sign (paved).

1.1   Turn **right** on **ROUTE 705** (paved).

1.2   **Route 705** changes to dirt (unpaved).

3.2   Stay **straight** on **ROUTE 705** at this intersection. Route 706 turns right.

3.4   Stay **right** on **ROUTE 705** at this intersection. Route 706 turns left.

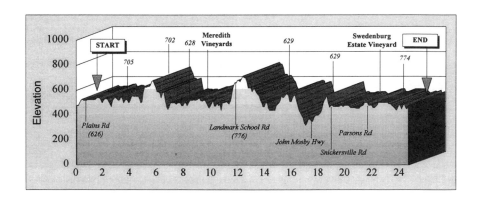

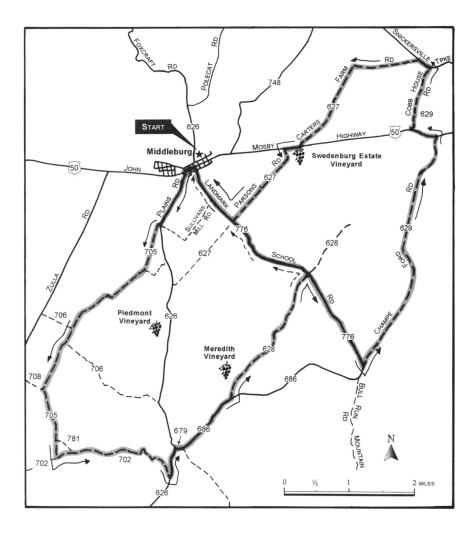

4.2 Turn **left** at the T, continuing on **ROUTE 705**. Route 708 goes right (unpaved).

5.3 Turn **left** at the stop sign on **ROUTE 702** (unpaved).

7.6 Turn **left** on **ROUTE 626** (paved).

7.9 Bear **right** on **ROUTE 679** at the bottom of the descent. This turns into **ROUTE 628**.

9.1 Turn **left** on **ROUTE 628**. This is slightly hidden. The turn is after a long rock wall on the left, just past a large brick house with three chimneys (unpaved).

9.4   **Meredith Vineyards** on the left. Stop in for a tour. Hours are from 10 A.M. to 4 P.M.

11.5   Turn **right** on **LANDMARK SCHOOL ROAD (ROUTE 776)** (paved).

For those who have had enough, you can turn **left** on **Landmark School Road** and take the shortcut back to Middleburg. 2.4 miles.

13.2   Turn **left** on **CHAMPE FORD ROAD (ROUTE 629)** (unpaved).

17.1   Turn **left** on **JOHN MOSBY HIGHWAY (ROUTE 50)**. Be careful of traffic (paved).

17.5   Turn **right** on **COBB HOUSE ROAD (ROUTE 629)** (unpaved).

18.5   Turn **left** on **SNICKERSVILLE ROAD** (paved).

Ride Information

Wine Tasting Hotline:

Meredith Vineyard	*(703) 687-6277*
Piedmont Vineyard	*(703) 687-5528*
Swedenburg Estate Vineyard	*(703) 687-5219*

Schedule:

Meredith Vineyard	*10–5, 7 days a week – N/C*
Piedmont Vineyard	*10–5, 7 days a week – N/C*
Swedenburg Estate Vineyard	*10 or more only – $2.00*

Maps:

USGS maps:	*Rectortown, VA; Middleburg, VA*
ADC maps:	*Loudoun County road map*
	Fauquier County road map

18.8   Turn **left** at the bottom of the hill on **CARTERS FARM ROAD (ROUTE 627)** (unpaved).

21.3   Turn **right** on **JOHN MOSBY HIGHWAY (ROUTE 50)** (paved).

Pass **Swedenburg Estate Vineyard**. Stop for a sip of wine before continuing on.

21.5   Turn **left** on **PARSONS ROAD (ROUTE 627)** (unpaved).

22.6   Turn **right** on **LANDMARK SCHOOL ROAD (ROUTE 776)** (paved).

23.0   Arrive back in Middleburg. Cross **Washington Street** to **MADISON STREET**.

23.1   Turn **right** into the school parking lot. Drink too much wine?

19. Old Waterford Dirt Ride

Start: *Loudoun Co. High School*	**Terrain:** *Rolling, dirt/gravel roads*
Length: *27.5 miles*	**Riding Time:** *2+ hours*
Rating: *Moderate to Difficult*	**Calories Burned:** *1200 – 2000*

When Amos Janney lead a small group of Quakers in 1733 from Bucks County, Pennsylvania, to the fertile land just west of the Catoctin Mountain along South Fork Creek, he may never have imagined that the land he sought would someday become Virginia's most beautiful horse country, and more significantly for cyclists, the ideal setting for some exceptionally scenic mountain bike rides.

But perhaps he did sense in some way what would become of the land he was settling. He and his group of Quakers yearned to be free of the persecutions of the "Old World" and to escape Pennsylvania's ever-increasing population. They sought the solitude and peace of this expansive valley between Catoctin and the Blue Ridge. Had this band of Quaker pioneers existed today, it's quite possible that their clothes, while still black, would be skin tight and made to breathe during a long bicycle ride in the summer heat.

It may be said that Mr. Janney laid the groundwork for mountain biking in this area. Unpaved roads, built since his time, climb along Catoctin Mountain, then roll leisurely along the valley floor. Panoramic views of the green countryside and the mountains

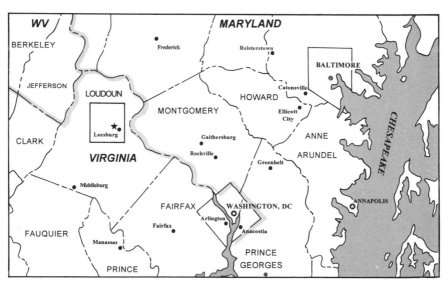

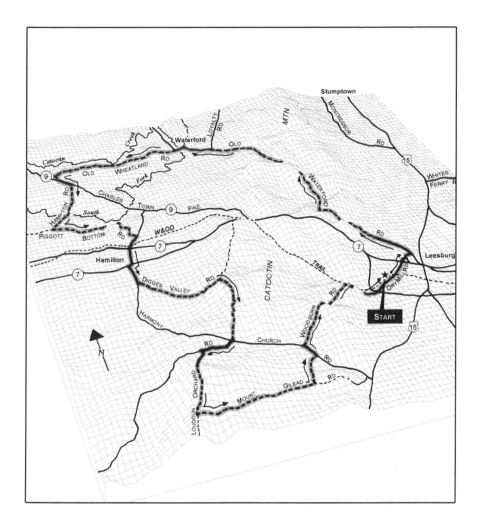

beyond are a wonderful backdrop to the horse and dairy farms spread throughout the valley. The Waterford-Hamilton-Leesburg area, just as Amos Janney and his group of settlers discovered, is the perfect location to escape the masses, to be free of the oppressive daily grind of our "New World," and to discover an undisturbed, peaceful haven.

The roads are primarily unpaved dirt and gravel roads perfect for the off-road tourist looking for more than ballistic singletrack and rugged trails. Stop in the historic town of Waterford, settled by Amos Janney as Milltown, then renamed by a little Irish cobbler whose hometown was Waterford, Ireland. Cross the Washington & Old Dominion Trail into the town of Hamilton for a little break, then be on your way, heading south toward Mt. Gilead before riding north again

(continued on page 157)

Old Waterford Dirt Ride

☞   **From the Capital Beltway (495)** – Take Exit 10, **Route 7 west (Leesburg Pike)** all the way to **Leesburg** (28 miles). At the **Leesburg city limits,** stay on **BUS Route 7**, Market Street through Leesburg. Turn **left** on **Catoctin Circle**, then, at the **third light**, turn **left** on **Dry Mill Road**. **Loudoun County High School** is on your right. Park here.

MILES DIRECTIONS

0.0 **START** at the **Loudon County High School** parking lot off Dry Mill Road. Turn **left** on **DRY MILL ROAD**. Follow the yellow bike route signs (paved).

0.3 Cross over **W&OD trail**. Continue **straight**.

0.5 Straight across **Loudoun Road**.

0.6 Cross **Market Street**.

0.7 Turn **right** on **CORNWAL STREET** (paved).

0.8 Turn **left** on **MEMORIAL DRIVE**. Memorial Drive stays to the right side of Memorial Hospital, heading toward Gibson Street (paved).

0.9 Turn **right** on **GIBSON STREET** (paved).

1.1 Turn **left** on **OLD WATERFORD ROAD** (paved). Graveyard on the right.

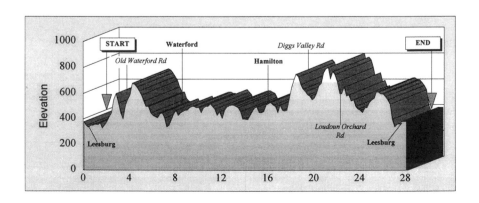

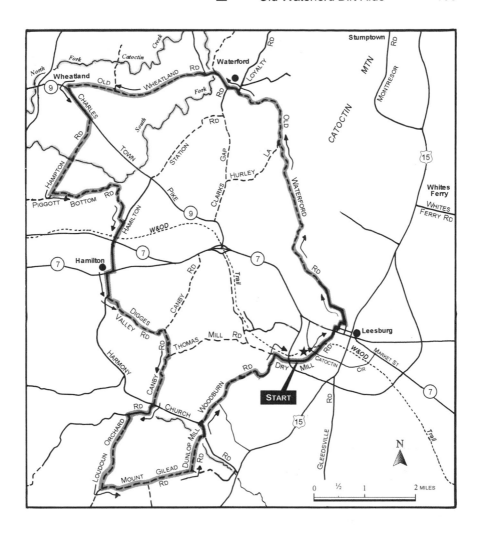

2.3 Old Waterford Road turns to gravel (unpaved).

5.3 Stay **right** at the intersection with Hurley Lane on **OLD WATERFORD ROAD** (unpaved).

7.2 Turn **left** on **MAIN WATER STREET** (paved).

Arrive in the historic town of **Waterford**.

7.4 Turn **left** on **OLD WHEATLAND ROAD** (paved).

7.7 **Old Wheatland Road** turns to gravel (unpaved).

10.6   Turn **left** on **CHARLES TOWN PIKE (VA ROUTE 9)** (paved).

Be careful along this road. The speed limit for cars is 55 mph.

11.2   Turn **right** on **HAMPTON ROAD** (unpaved).

11.8   Turn **left** on **PIGGOTT BOTTOM ROAD** (unpaved).

12.2   Bear **left** at the stop sign, continuing on **PIGGOTT BOT-TOM ROAD**.

14.0   Turn **right** on **HAMILTON STATION ROAD** (paved).

14.3   Cross **W&OD trail**.

15.1   Turn **right** on **COLONIAL HIGHWAY** (paved).

Arrive in the historic town of **Hamilton**.

15.2   Turn **left** on **HARMONY CHURCH ROAD** (paved).

Ride Information

Trail Maintenance Hotline:
> *None available*

Schedule:
> *None available*

Maps:
> USGS maps: *Purcellville, VA; Lincoln, VA*
> *Leesburg, VA; Waterford, VA*
> ADC maps: *Loudoun County road map*

(continued from page153)

to Leesburg. Be sure to notice the spectacular homes along Loudoun Orchard Road and Mount Gilead Road, and be careful not to bump into the deer residing in force throughout this area.

15.8   Bear **left** on **DIGGS VALLEY ROAD** (unpaved).

17.2   Diggs Valley Road comes to a four-way intersection. Turn **left**, continuing on **DIGGS VALLEY ROAD** (unpaved).

17.4   Turn **right** on **CANBY ROAD** (unpaved). Stay on Canby all the way to Harmony Church Road.

19.0   Cross **Harmony Church Road** to **LOUDOUN ORCHARD ROAD** (paved).

19.7   Bear **left**, continuing on **LOUDOUN ORCHARD ROAD** (paved).

20.1   Loudoun Orchard Road turns to gravel (unpaved).

21.4   Turn **left** on **MOUNT GILEAD ROAD** (unpaved).

23.3   Turn **left** on **DUNLOP MILL ROAD** (unpaved).

24.1   Turn **left** on **HARMONY CHURCH ROAD** (paved).

24.3   Turn **right** on **WOODBURN ROAD** (unpaved).

26.7   Turn **right** on **DRY MILL ROAD**.

27.5   Arrive at **Loudoun County High School**.

20. Ball's Bluff Canal Ride

Start: *Ball's Bluff Battlefield*	**Terrain:** *Dirt roads, C&O Canal*
Length: *31.1 miles*	**Riding Time:** *2½ – 3½ hours*
Rating: *Difficult*	**Calories Burned:** *2000 – 3000*

Following what he believed were instructions from General George McClellan to push south, Union General Stone set in motion a series of events on the night of October 20, 1861, that would result the next evening in carnage on the wooded bluff above the Potomac River.

Reconnaissance reported to General Stone an ill-guarded Confederate camp outside Leesburg, Virginia. Eager for the opportunity to destroy it, Stone positioned his men at Conrad's (Whites) Ferry, Harrisons Island, and Edwards Ferry. Movement across the swollen Potomac began at midnight, but Stone's men found no camp at the reported site. They found, instead, only a moonlit grove of trees, mistaken by his men the previous night as tents.

They chose to continue toward Leesburg and, early that morning, met resistance from a Confederate outpost just north of Leesburg near Ball's Bluff. After hearing of skirmishes with Union soldiers, four companies of Confederate infantry were sent from Leesburg to the previously small outpost just west of Ball's Bluff, pushing the Union troops back toward the river. Throughout the

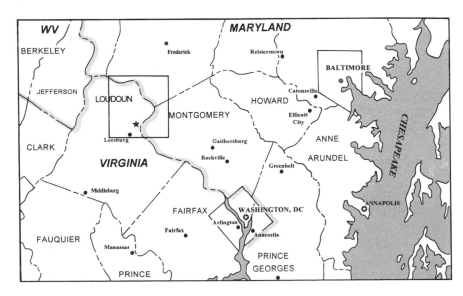

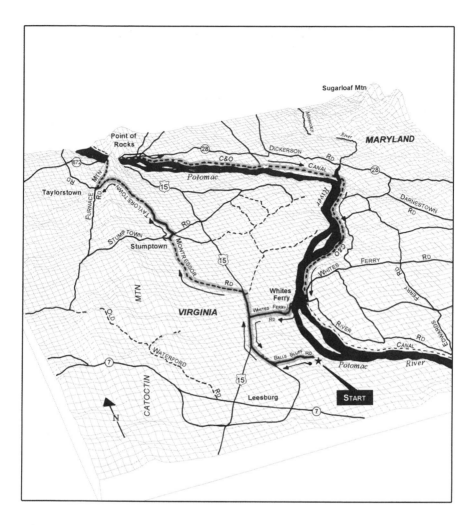

afternoon, a series of advancements and attacks by a continually reinforced Confederate line forced the ill-fated Union troops near the edge of a steep drop to the rocky banks of the Potomac. When Union reinforcement did arrive by climbing a path at the side of the bluff, there was confusion among the officers over who was in command. A decision finally was made to fight their way through Confederate lines, since the only alternative was to retreat off the bluff, 90 feet down to the river below. But just as the Union attempted their advance, Confederates launched a murderous attack, blocking both the path that Union reinforcements had previously climbed and any chance for their retreat. Federal troops were suddenly forced to choose between furious Confederate gunfire or a suicidal leap to the

(continued on page 163)

Ball's Bluff Canal Ride

☞   **From the Capital Beltway (495)** – Take Exit 10, **Route 7 west (Leesburg Pike)** all the way to **Leesburg** (28 miles). At the Leesburg city limits, take **Route 15 north** for approximately 1.5 miles, then turn **right** on **Ball's Bluff Road**. This will take you 0.8 miles to **Ball's Bluff National Cemetery and Battlefield**. Park here and begin your ride.

MILES   DIRECTIONS

0.0   **START** at **Ball's Bluff Battlefield Regional Park**. Follow **BALL'S BLUFF ROAD** to **Route 15 (Leesburg Pike)**.

1.0   Turn **right** on **ROUTE 15 North (LEESBURG PIKE)**. Ride on the shoulder.

4.1   Turn **left** on **MONTRESSOR ROAD (ROUTE 661)** (unpaved).

5.0   Bear **right**, continuing on **MONTRESSOR ROAD**.

7.2   Turn **right** on **STUMPTOWN ROAD (ROUTE 662)** (paved).

7.7   Turn **left** on **NEWVALLEY CHURCH ROAD (ROUTE 663)** (paved).

8.2   Turn **right** on **TAYLORSTOWN ROAD (ROUTE 663)** (paved).

9.9   **Taylorstown Road** turns to gravel and begins a steep ascent (unpaved).

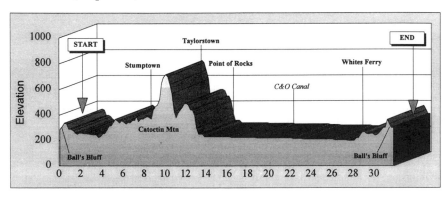

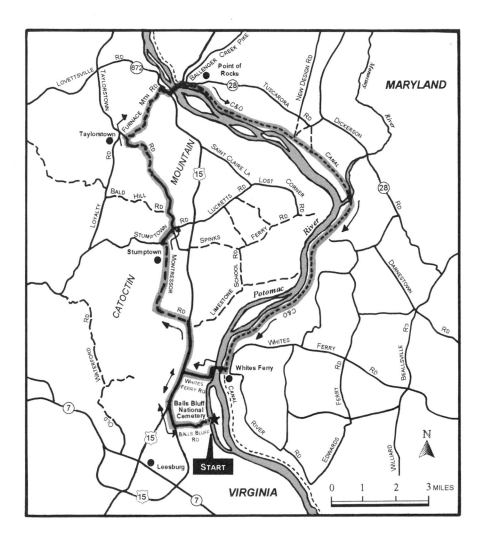

10.7   Reach the summit of this climb.   Begin a fast, gravelly descent.

11.3   Turn **right** on **FURNACE MOUNTAIN ROAD (ROUTE 665)** at the bottom of the descent (unpaved).

Continue straight at this turn 0.2 miles to Taylorstown for food.

13.7   Turn **right** on **LOVETTSVILLE ROAD (ROUTE 672)** (paved).

13.75   Turn **left** on **ROUTE 15 North** and cross the bridge over the Potomac. (Use the sidewalk to cross the bridge.)

14.3   Once across the bridge, turn **right** on **ROUTE 28** (paved) into **POINT OF ROCKS, MD**. There's a general store one block up the road.

Turn **right** immediately on **COMMERCE STREET**. (This is a small street that goes behind the houses on Main Street.) Follow this across the railroad track, then over the wooden bridge to the **C&O Canal towpath** (paved).

14.4   Turn **left** on the **C&O CANAL TOWPATH**, heading downriver (unpaved).

27.1   Turn **right** on **WHITES FERRY ROAD** to **Whites Ferry** (paved).

Take the ferry across the Potomac. Remember to bring toll money (50¢ for bicycles).

28.4   Turn **left** on **ROUTE 15 South (JAMES MONROE HIGHWAY)** (paved – ride on the shoulder).

Ride Information

Trail Maintenance Hotline:

C&O Canal headquarters   (301) 739-4200

Cost:

Whites Ferry – 50¢ for bicycles, $2.00 for cars

Schedule:

Ball's Bluff National Cemetery is open from dawn till dusk
Whites Ferry is open from 6 A.M. to 11 P.M. every day

Maps:

USGS maps: Leesburg, VA; Waterford, VA
                Point of Rocks, MD; Poolesville, MD

ADC maps: Loudoun Co., VA; Montgomery Co., MD

30.1   Turn **left** on **BALL'S BLUFF ROAD** toward the battlefield (paved).

31.1   Arrive back at **Ball's Bluff National Battlefield**.

(continued from page 159)

rocks far below. Nearly 1,000 Union soldiers were lost that afternoon, dealing a severe blow to the North, which was still reeling from its recent defeat at the first Battle of Bull Run. Ball's Bluff National Cemetery and Battlefield, the country's smallest national battlefield, remains today a quiet testimony to America's most violent era.

This ride, which begins at Ball's Bluff, offers a real variation in terrain to cyclists. Traveling first in Virginia, the course alternates between paved and unpaved roads, starting out flat, then rolling, before getting very hilly as it crosses over Catoctin Mountain. On the Maryland side, you can relax along the all-flat, all-dirt C&O Canal towpath which meanders along the scenic Potomac River. Along the way, you will cross over the Monocacy Aqueduct, the largest aqueduct along the 185-mile canal. Catch the ferry at Whites Ferry to cross back over to the Virginia side, then return to the start of the ride.

21. South Run Power Lines

Start: *South Run Park*	**Terrain:** *Hilly singletrack/pavement*
Length: *10.1 miles*	**Riding Time:** *1 – 2 hours*
Rating: *Difficult*	**Calories Burned:** *1000 – 2000*

Many of you may never have considered that the electric company would have anything to do with creating some of the most challenging and rugged mountain biking terrain anywhere. As this and the following ride reveal, off-road cycling just doesn't get any better than this.

They zap and crackle nearly 60 feet above you, and you wonder just how many volts *are* rushing at light speed through those high-voltage wires. But is this of any consequence when you have miles of twisting, rugged trails through what resembles a linear wasteland?

Power lines — ideal bike lanes *(for a mountain bike)* exist everywhere. Electric companies have often permitted and even encouraged the use of their land beneath these high-voltage giants for such things as linear parks, equestrian trails, and hiker-biker paths (ie. sections of the Washington & Old Dominion Trail). However, not all land beneath the power lines is accessible to the public, and this must be understood.

All the power lines you see stretch over private property,

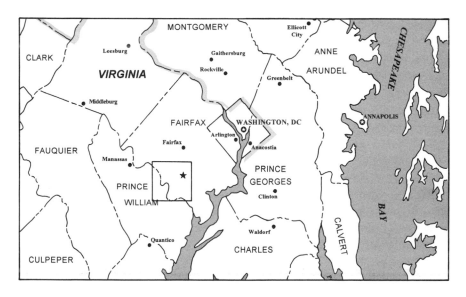

whether owned by the power company themselves or individual land owners. In many cases, these lines cross property where trespassing is taken very seriously. Do not ride through these areas! Fortunately, it's usually easy to tell what areas are strictly off-limits. For example, when power lines cross a farmer's soybean field or over someone's backyard, this land is not a place to ride your bike. It's also easy to recognize whether the trail is fit for riding. Not all land beneath the power lines is maintained for easy access, and often this land becomes so overgrown with thorny weeds and razor-sharp sawgrass that riding would be more a blood bath than a good time. Some land, though, is just right for a challenging and exciting off-road experience. These places have few, if any, points of contention in regard to

(continued on page 169)

South Run Power Lines

☞   **From the Beltway (495)** – take **I-95 south** toward Richmond. Go only about 0.5 miles to the Springfield **Exit 57, Route 644 west (Old Keene Mill Road)**. Follow **Old Keene Mill Road** west 4 miles, then turn **left** on **Huntsman Boulevard**. Follow Huntsman Boulevard 1.5 miles to Pohick Road. Turn **right** on **Pohick Road**, go about 0.3 miles, and turn **left** into **South Run District Park**. Parking, water, telephones, toilets, showers available.

MILES   DIRECTIONS

0.0   **START** at the **South Run Recreation Center**, behind the main building and field house. Follow the paved path from the rear parking area down into the woods.

0.2   At the bottom of the hill, follow the **ASPHALT PATH** to the **right** along South Run.

0.4   Reach the **power lines**. Turn **left**, crossing South Run stream, and travel **south** along the **dirt trail** beneath the **POWER LINES**.

0.8   The power lines cross **Chapel Oak Court** and **Oak Bridge Place,** heading toward **Route 123**. Follow the power lines aross **Route 123 (Ox Road)**.

1.2   Cross the **gas pipeline**. Continue **straight**.

2.0   Continue past the enormous **power station** on your left.

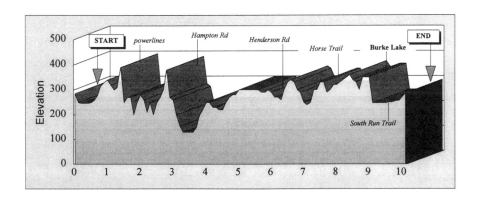

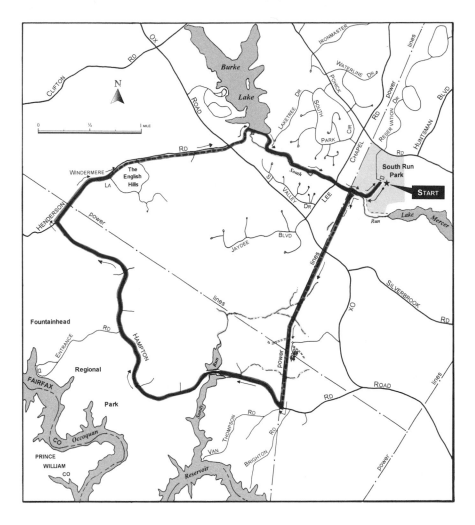

2.7   Turn **right** on **HAMPTON ROAD** toward Fountainhead park (paved).

4.9   Reach **Fountainhead Park** entrance. Turn left to go down to the marina and concessions building.

- **FOOD.** 0.8 miles to the marina and concession stand. There is a network of wooded hiking trails within Fountainhead Park. They are explicitly prohibited to bicycles, however. These trails will take you all the way up to Bull Run Park.

6.3   Turn **right** on **HENDERSON ROAD**.

7.1   At the intersection of **Henderson Road** and **Windermere Lane**, turn off the road by the brick **English Hills** subdivision sign, and hop on the **EQUESTRIAN TRAIL** paralleling the right side of Henderson Road. This trail goes all the way to Route 123 (Ox Road).

8.3   Cross **Route 123 (Ox Road)** to the **SINGLETRACK TRAIL** directly across from Henderson Road. (Look just inches to the **right** of the yellow directional sign. The trail begins here.) Be very careful crossing Route 123. The traffic is often very heavy.

8.4   Bear **right** at the fork in the trail.

8.6   Arrive at **Burke Lake Dam**. Turn **right**, traveling across the dam.

8.8   Once across the dam, turn **right** on the **ASPHALT TRAIL,** leading you away from the lake. This takes you back to **South Run Park**. (You could turn left and follow this dirt path all the way around the lake. Approximately five miles around.)

Ride Information

Trail Maintenance Hotline:

South Run Recreation Center   (703) 644-7070

Fairfax County Park Authority   (703) 246-5741

Schedule:

South Run Recreation Center   6 A.M. – 9 P.M., 7 days a week

Maps:

USGS maps: Fairfax, VA; Occoquan, VA

ADC maps: Northern Virginia road map

9.7 Cross underneath **Lee Chapel Road**.

9.9 Cross the **power lines**. Continue straight along asphalt path.

10.1 Arrive back at **South Run Park**.

(continued from page 165)

trespassing. And the terrain, while resembling something from a *Mad Max* movie, has negotiable singletrack or jeep trails from which you can emerge unscathed by the vicious prickers.

The two rides in this book are of the latter type of power-line riding, and both offer a tremendous adventure for any singletrack junky. It's important also to realize that on these rides there is always a way forward. Part of the challenge along these rugged trails is the constant presence of obstacles, whether it be rocks, logs, stream crossings, or thick mud. All of this, though, is nothing but good, clean fun.

This ride follows the power lines south from South Run Park to Hampton Road. Although you must travel pavement along the second part of this ride, traffic is light and scenery fantastic. Zoning in this area is five acres *minimum*, so houses and lots tend to be both beautiful and enormous. Hampton Road winds its way along the wooded lane alongside Fountainhead Regional Park in which nature trails take hikers more than 18 miles to Bull Run, near the Manassas National Battlefield. You then pick up an equestrian trail paralleling Henderson Road as you continue to roll past million-dollar estates. The route takes a fun little trail through the woods at Route 123, then up to Burke Lake Dam for an incredible view of Northern Virginia's largest lake. If you're up to it, follow the dirt bike path around the lake. Otherwise, take the asphalt path back to South Run Park, and ask yourself how *you* might one day own a house like those along Hampton and Henderson Road.

22. Centreville Power Lines

Start: *Mount Olive Church*	**Terrain:** *Rugged singletrack*
Length: *7.8 miles*	**Riding Time:** *1–1½ hours*
Rating: *Difficult*	**Calories Burned:** *1000–1500*

Centreville had been trying to grow for some time — but was having a tough time of it. Since its establishment in 1792, this small trading center, located nearly equidistant from Leesburg, Warrenton, Middleburg, Washington, Georgetown, and Alexandria, had tried diligently to become more than just a rest stop along Braddock Road.

When construction began on Little River Turnpike in the late eighteenth century, the town hoped this trade highway, stretching west from Alexandria, would be built to pass through their community. Alexandria was, at the time, the Potomac's largest market town. Developers, however, routed the Little River Turnpike north in favor of smoother, more even terrain, bypassing the town altogether. The town later tried to house the District Court of Virginia, which served Fairfax, Fauquier, Loudoun, and Prince William Counties. This idea was rejected in favor of Dumfries in Prince William County. Ever persistent, Centreville founded what it hoped would become a prestigious academy to attract outside scholars to take up residence in local homes. This also went without much success. At one time, Centreville was even known as a local center for slave rental and trade.

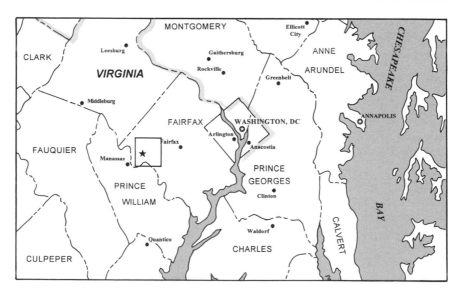

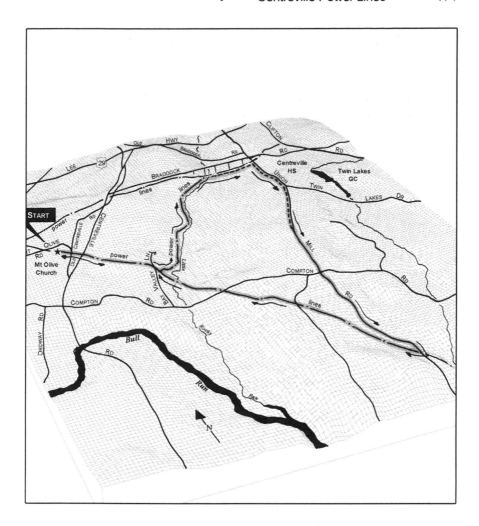

But into the twentieth century, this small town remained nothing more than the unimposing rest stop it had always been.

As you pass through Centreville today, however, much of this history may seem distant and unfamiliar, because the town has suddenly become a sprawling community of subdivisions, shopping centers, and beltway commuters. And it continues to expand at a phenomenal rate further and further west.

Centreville is not unlike many communities surrounding the Washington-Baltimore area that have, in the last 10 to 20 years, had tremendous growth spurts. This explosive growth has, in most cases, virtually wiped out the small-town flavor that dominated the region west of the cities. Towns and villages, desperate for so long to attract

(continued on page 175)

Centreville Power Lines

☞   From Rte 66 – Exit **South** on **Rte 28 (Sully Road)**. Sully Road changes to **Centreville Road**. Follow **Centreville Road** 1.5 miles, then turn **right** on **Old Centreville Road**. Go 0.5 miles to **Mount Olive Church** on the right to park and begin the ride.

MILES   DIRECTIONS

0.0   **START** at **Mount Olive Church** parking lot and follow the **POWER LINES east** toward Centreville Road.   Cross **Centreville Road** at the light, then resume the **POWER LINES**. Follow the trail on the **left side**.

0.75   Cross **Bay Valley Lane**.

0.8   Turn **left** at the small fenced-in substation, following the secondary **POWER LINES** that run along **Little Rocky Run Creek** to Braddock Road.

2.0   Pass a small park with tennis courts.

2.2   Reenter the trail on the **right side** of the **POWER LINES** after passing the park.

2.4   Climb up the embankment at **Braddock Road** and turn **right** on the **ASPHALT PATH**. At this point, the trail beneath the power lines disapppears as the power lines parallel Braddock Road.

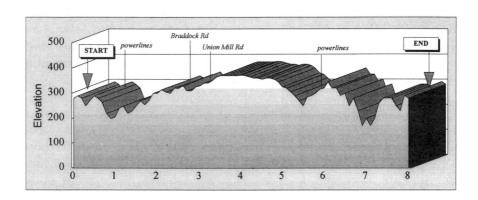

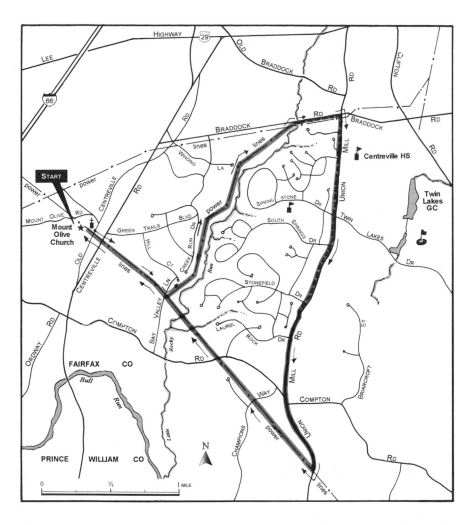

2.8 Turn **right** on the asphalt **BIKE PATH** along **Union Mill Road**.

3.1 Centreville High School on the left.

4.3 Bike path ends. Continue riding along the shoulder. Be careful of traffic.

4.8 At this intersection, go straight through the stop sign. Compton Road bears a sharp left. Stay straight here and ride past the sign that says **"DEAD END,"** continuing on Union Mill Road.

5.3   Turn **right** off **Union Mill Road**, and ride down the steep ditch to the **POWER LINES**, and head **west** back to Centreville Road.

6.4   Cross **Compton Road**.

7.0   Pass the small fenced-in power station on the right. Continue straight. Cross **Bay Valley Lane**.

7.7   Reach **Centreville Road**. Cross at the light.

7.8   Arrive back at **Mount Olive Church**. Tough ride!

Ride Information

Trail Maintenance Hotline:
   Not available

Schedule:
   Not available

Maps:
   USGS maps: *Manassas, VA*
   ADC maps: *Northern Virginia road map*

Trails abound beneath the power lines

(continued from page 171)

more people and new businesses, could never have anticipated the recent boom in development, which has turned these small hamlets into huge bedroom communities for the Washington-Baltimore megalopolis.

   With this growth, precious back roads and trails were permanently lost, forcing cyclists to look even harder for new places to ride. Thus, the discovery of the power lines! They may not be scenic mountain roads with heavenly vistas, but the rugged trails beneath these crackling wires make for the ultimate off-road adventure. They have it all — rocks, ditches, hills, dirt, and most importantly, open land on which to ride. You'll find yourself crashing down rocky descents, slogging through muddy streambeds, then up and over steep, rutted climbs that snake back and forth beneath the supercharged black cables.

   The most important thing to remember when riding the power lines is there is *always* a way through the obstacles. Sometimes you just have to find it. Have fun!

23. Glade to Great Falls

Start: *Colts Neck Rec Area*	**Terrain:** *Singletrack trails/bike path*
Length: *30 miles round trip*	**Riding Time:** *2½ – 3 hours round trip*
Rating: *Moderate*	**Calories Burned:** *1500 – 2000*

     This 15-mile route from Reston, Virginia, to Great Falls National Park may define what is becoming a new kind of trailway through growing suburban landscapes. Combining a mixture of clay-surfaced singletrack, bike paths, public parkland, and creek corridors, this ride follows what is perhaps the longest, most unique trail system in the region.

     The first half of the ride weaves its way through Reston, Virginia, once a leader in community planning. One feature setting this small city apart is its intricate network of public walkways, designed to take you in any direction without having to get on the roads. The ride starts along The Glade, a trickling creek at the southern edge of the Reston development, through Glade Stream Valley Park. You can choose to ride on a natural-surface trail or an asphalt path, both of which parallel the creek for three miles. This trail changes over to an all-dirt singletrack along Twin Branches Trail, then takes you to the Washington & Old Dominion Railroad Trail. Turn left on the W&OD and follow it for a few miles to Michael Faraday Court, where another trail, beginning at the end of the court, takes you

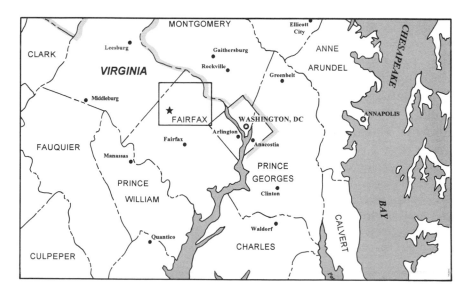

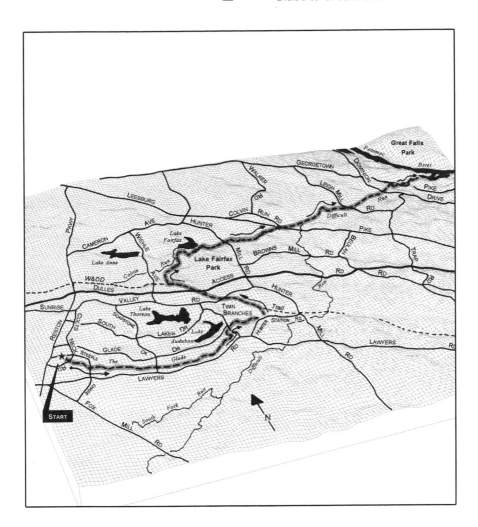

winding along Colvin Run through Lake Fairfax Park. You may wish to stop for lunch at this 479-acre park and enjoy the beautiful lake, take a train ride, or even go for a swim. Down the hill to the southeast side of the park, the trail resumes its course along Colvin Run, well marked for horseback riding. It then continues east across Leesburg Pike to Difficult Run. The trail comes to a scenic ending at the Potomac River in Great Falls National Park, where you can watch the turbulent water rushing through Mather Gorge.

Please be aware of the rapidly deteriorating conditions of the trailway along Difficult Run. In recent years, this scenic, wooded path tracing the banks of the creek has been transformed into a muddy bog, slogging its way along a course of disaster for anyone hoping to use

(continued on page 182)

Glade to Great Falls

☞   From the **Capital Beltway (495)** – Take the **Washington-Dulles Access Road** (toll road) west for 8 miles to **Exit 3, Reston Parkway**. Go **south** on **Reston Parkway** 1.7 miles, then turn **left** on **Colts Neck Road**. Go 0.4 miles just past Stirrup Road (on the right), then turn **left** into a small gravel **parking lot** at the neighborhood **tennis court**. Park here.

MILES   DIRECTIONS

0.0   **START** from the tennis court parking lot on **Colts Neck Road**. Cross **Colts Neck Road** and follow the **ASPHALT PATH** on the **left side** of the guard rail into **Glade Stream Valley Park**.

0.4   Cross **Steeplechase Road**. Continue on the **ASPHALT PATH**.

0.5   Bear **right** on the natural-surface trail, continuing along the Glade. This **NATURAL-SURFACE TRAIL** parallels an asphalt path all the way to Twin Branches Road. Ride the one you're most comfortable with.

1.0   Go straight across a small playground with a basketball court. **NATURAL-SURFACE TRAIL** continues straight ahead.

1.3   Cross **Soapstone Road**.

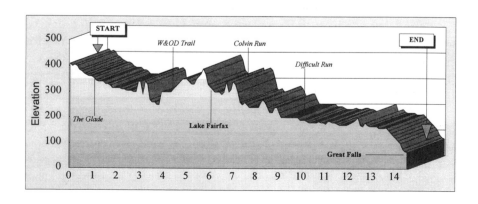

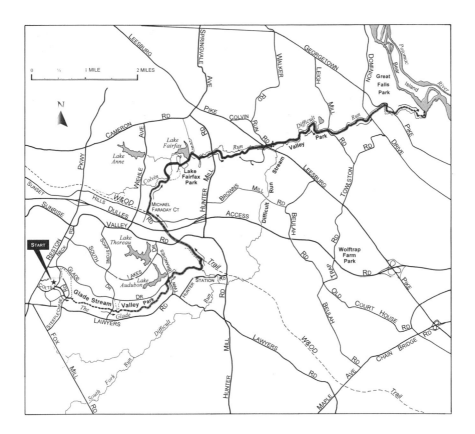

2.8 Cross **Twin Branches Road**. Follow **TWIN BRANCHES NATURE TRAIL** into the woods.

3.6 Trail comes to a T and the creek splits. Turn **left**, going toward the W&OD Bike Trail.

3.7 Bear **right** toward **W&OD Bike Trail** from Twin Branches Trail. Turn **left** on the **W&OD BIKE TRAIL**.

4.8 Cross **Sunrise Valley Drive**.

5.1 Go underneath **Dulles Access Road**.

5.4   Cross **Sunset Hills Road.**

5.7   Turn **right** into **MICHAEL FARADAY COURT.** Go to the end of the court where a dirt trail takes you up the small grassy hill into Reston Industrial Park, then to **COLVIN RUN TRAIL**, along Colvin Run.

6.6   **Colvin Run Trail** comes to a trail intersection. Turn **left**, following the **LAKE FAIRFAX NATURE TRAIL** up to the camping grounds and playing fields of Lake Fairfax.

7.1   Turn **right** up the **GRAVEL ROAD** to the playing fields. Playing fields on the right, group camping on the left. Follow the gravel road to Lake Fairfax Dam.

7.5   Cross **Lake Fairfax Dam** into the main park area. This is a popular park, complete with food, drinks, bathrooms, working train, and park office. It's also a good place for a lunch break. Then follow the **HORSE TRAIL**, beginning in front of the park office, down the hill south of the dam and back toward Colvin Run.

8.3   Cross **Hunter Mill Road.** Once across this road, follow the marked **HORSE TRAIL (white blaze with horseshoe)** along Colvin Run. This trail takes you all the way to Great Falls National Park.

9.5   Trail drops you out on **Carpers Farm Way.** Turn **left** on **CARPERS FARM WAY** to the light at **Leesburg Pike (Route 7).** Cross **Leesburg Pike**, then turn immediately **right**, following this unimproved road to its end.

— WARNING —

You must cross Difficult Run a number of times in this last section. If you would rather stay dry, then turn around before it's too late!

HELP!

The following section of trail along Difficult Creek to Great Falls is in great need of attention.

• Avoid riding here when the ground may be wet, espe-

cially after a rain storm or during the thawing season.
- Always stay on the trail. It's better to walk your bike through the muddy sections than to ride around them, thus widening the trail even further.
- Get involved to repair and maintain this unique off-road trail.

9.7 Follow the **HORSE TRAIL** (**white blaze**) at the end of this road. This leads you along Difficult Run toward the Potomac.

10.3 Cross **Difficult Run**. The trail continues on the other side of the creek.

11.3 Cross **Leigh Mill Road**. Continue straight on **DIFFICULT RUN TRAIL**. Equestrian park on the right.

13.0 Cross at the low point in the creek from the right side of Difficult Run to the left side. Otherwise, the trail along the right side of the creek ends.

13.4 Go underneath **Old Dominion Road**. Enter **Great Falls National Park**.

13.6 Cross Difficult Run again. Smooth concrete layers the creek bottom here. Be careful crossing here.

13.8 Cross Difficult Run.

14.0 Cross Difficult Run one last time. Follow Difficult Run to the **right**, which takes you underneath **Georgetown Pike**, and continues to the Potomac.

14.8 Reach the Potomac River at the southern end of Mather Gorge.

There is a great network of trails through Great Falls all of which are open to bikes. Look to ride #16 for maps of Great Falls National Park.

(continued from page 177)

this creek corridor in the future. Be very delicate on this trail, and ride only when the ground is dry. Your help in preserving this trail will stand to benefit *everyone* in years to come. Contact the Fairfax County or National Park Service to help maintain the trail, then gather a group of friends together on a Saturday afternoon and, with park-service guidance, put some sweat back into the trail.

Ride Information

Trail Maintenance Hotline:

Fairfax County Park Service	*(703) 246-5741*
National Park Service	*(703) 759-2915*
Reston Association (The Glade)	*(703) 437-7658*

Schedule:

Parks and trails open from dawn until dusk

Maps:

USGS maps: Vienna, VA; Falls Church, VA
ADC maps: Northern Virginia road map
Lake Fairfax Park and Trail map
Great Falls map and trail guide
Reston Pathways & Facilities Map

Fletcher Harris

Members of M.O.R.E. (Mid-Atlantic Off Road Enthusiasts) work with a park official to repair a section of trail. M.O.R.E. is regularly involved with trail repair, maintenance, and preservation both locally and throughout the Mid-Atlantic. They're always looking for more help. Get involved! (703) 631-2023

24. Fort Circle Trail

Start: *Smithsonian/Fort Stanton*	**Terrain:** *Hilly singletrack, gravel*
Length: *12.2 miles round trip*	**Riding Time:** *1 – 2 hours round trip*
Rating: *Difficult*	**Calories Burned:** *1000 – 2000*

After Confederates overwhelmingly defeated the Union army at the first battle of Manassas in July 1861, Union General George McClellan, aware of Washington's vulnerability, ordered heavy fortifications built around the virtually defenseless Union capital. Then, Fort Washington, nearly 12 miles down river, was all that guarded Washington. But by the spring of 1865, a ring of 68 forts, 93 batteries, and nearly 200 cannons and mortars surrounded the capital, making it the most heavily fortified city in the nation.

The only challenge to Washington's defenses came in July 1864, with a daring attack by Confederate General Jubal A. Early. Choosing a route through the northern perimeter of the city's defense, Early fought his way from Frederick, Maryland, to Silver Spring. But Union forces rushed reinforcements to the northern garrisons above Washington and successfully routed Early's troops. The Confederates were forced to retreat across the Potomac at Whites Ferry and Edwards Ferry, ending the first and only action against the city.

Most of the forts and batteries were dismantled after the Civil War, and the land returned to its prewar owners. Nonetheless,

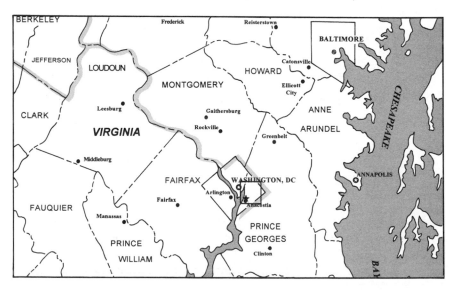

remains of several of these fortifications were preserved by the National Park Service and now make up what is known as the Fort Circle Parks. Among those under the care of the National Park Service are several forts built on hilltops overlooking the Anacostia River. Fort Mahan, Fort Chaplin, Fort Dupont, Fort Davis, and Fort Stanton were some of the strongholds guarding over Capitol Hill.

Today, the corridor between these forts along the Anacostia River makes a wonderful greenway, complete with a well-maintained and clearly marked hiker-biker trail that connects Fort Stanton with Fort Mahan. Long sections of narrow singletrack and twisting trails take you up and down the steep hills on which each fort was built. Cyclists, however, must allow plenty of daylight for this ride and

(continued on page 189)

Fort Circle Trail

☞   **From the Beltway (495)** – Exit **North** on **MD-Route 5 (Branch Avenue)** toward Washington. Go 2.8 miles, then turn **left** on **Suitland Parkway**. Go 1.8 miles, turn **right** at the light on **Stanton Road**. Take an immediate **right** up **Gainesville Street**, then **left** up **18th Street**. At the top of the hill, turn **right** on **Erie Street** and park at the **Smithsonian Museum of African-American History**. Telephone, water, toilets available.

☞   **From the Baltimore-Washington Parkway (Kenilworth Avenue/295)** – Exit **West** on **Suitland Parkway**. Go 1.2 miles, turn **left** at the first light on **Stanton Road**. Continue with directions above.

MILES   DIRECTIONS

0.0   **START** in the parking lot of Anacostia's Smithsonian Museum for African-American History. Cross **Erie Street** to the open grassy area opposite the parking lot. Staying right of the dirt road next to Fort Stanton Park's swimming pool, follow the **thin dirt path** diagonally across the field up into the woods. (Entrance into the woods is at the far right corner of the field.) Follow this trail into the woods no more than 20 feet before turning sharp **left** down a steep **single-track trail**.

0.2   End of descent. Cross the **wooden foot bridge** over the creek.

0.5   Cross **Good Hope Road**. Follow Park Service's **HIKER-**

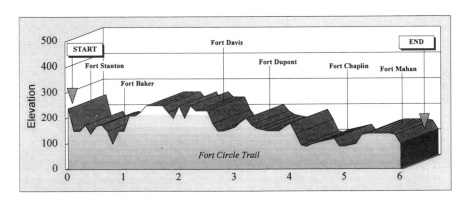

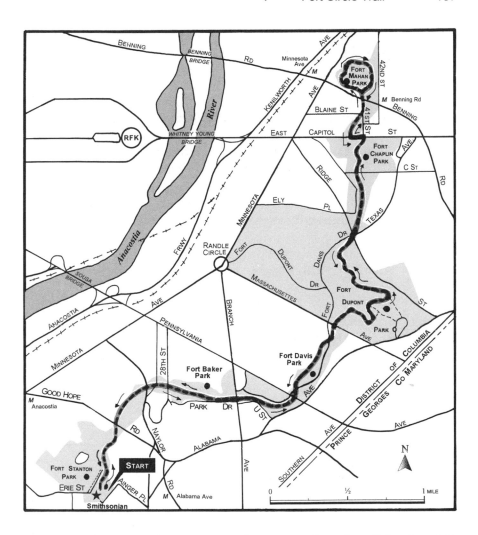

BIKER trail sign across the street. Paved trail for first 100 feet then changes back to dirt and gravel.

0.9   Cross **Naylor Avenue**. **HIKER-BIKER** trail is directly across the street, slightly to the right.

1.2   Cross **28th STREET, South East**.   **HIKER-BIKER** trail entrance is to the **left**.

1.6   Exit trail to **PARK DRIVE, South East,** and turn **left**. Follow this for one block to **Branch Avenue**. Cross Branch Avenue. **HIKER-BIKER** trail entrance is to the **left**.

2.1   Cross **Pennsylvania Avenue**. Entrance to **Fort Davis Park**. Bear **left** at the entrance, continuing on **HIKER-BIKER** trail down into the woods.

2.7   Trail turns into asphalt. Cross **Fort Davis Road**.

2.9   Cross **Massachusetts Avenue**. Continue straight on **HIKER-BIKER** trail (back to dirt/gravel). Enter **Fort Dupont Park**.

3.5   Trail forks. Turn **left** at the first fork, taking the **LOWER** trail. (**Right** will take you up to **Fort Dupont** — 0.5 miles.)

3.7   Trail comes to a **T**. Turn **left**, horseshoeing slightly downhill. **Ridge Road** should remain above you on your right.

4.4   Trail exits at the intersection of **Fort Davis Road** and **Ridge Road**. **HIKER-BIKER** trail sign is catty-corner across this intersection. Cross the **Fort Davis Road/Ridge Road** intersection. The trail entrance at this point is somewhat overgrown. Keep your eyes peeled.

Ride Information

Trail Maintenance Hotline:

National Capital Park East   (202) 426-7723
National Park Service   (202) 426-7745

Schedule:

Open from dawn until sunset every day of the year

Maps:

USGS maps: Washington East; Anacostia, DC, MD
ADC maps: Prince George's County
Fort Circle Parks historical map
Fort Dupont Park

4.9 Cross **C Street**. **HIKER-BIKER** trail entrance is to the **right**.

5.1 Trail splits. Bear **left** at this split.

5.2 Trail comes to a **T**. Turn **right**.

5.3 Cross **East Capitol Street**. Be careful of traffic. Take the crosswalk to the right. Then follow the **HIKER-BIKER** trail sign up the hill, back into the woods.

5.6 Exit trail to **41st STREET**.

5.7 Cross **Benning Street**. Go straight up the unmarked embankment to the asphalt path and turn **left**. Follow this trail around as it does a full circle around **Fort Mahan Park**.

6.6 Arrive back at **Benning Street** and **41st Street**. Follow the **HIKER-BIKER** trail signs back along the **Fort Circle Trail** to where you started at the Smithsonian's African-American History Museum.

(continued from page 185)

should study directions and maps carefully before starting. While the trail winds through a forested oasis, it's also in some of Washington's rougher neighborhoods notorious for their high crime rates. Be safe, wear your armor, and have fun, because this is absolutely one of Washington's greatest mountain bike rides!

25. C&O Canal

Start: *G-town Visitors Center*	**Terrain:** *Flat canal towpath*
Length: *184.5 miles one way*	**Riding Time:** *Varies w/distance*
Rating: *Easy*	**Calories Burned:** *Varies w/distance*

On a hot Fourth of July in Washington, D.C., 1828, ground was broken and the challenge under way to see who would reach the western "frontier" *(Wheeling, West Virginia)* first. The competitors — the Chesapeake & Ohio Canal Company versus the Baltimore & Ohio Railroad. Both started digging the same day. Through high costs, floods, land-access problems, 185 miles of rugged earth along the Potomac River, and 22 years of backbreaking labor, the C&O canal finally reached Cumberland, Maryland — eight years *after* the B&O. Nevertheless, 11 stone aqueducts, 74 lift locks, and 185 miles of canal were complete. *(The remainder of the route to Wheeling, West Virginia, would be by road.)* Unfortunately for the C&O, not only did the railroad reach the west first, but it was also faster and more reliable, as the canal was often handicapped by floods, freezes, and drought. Losing money to the railroad and regularly repairing costly flood damage, the C&O Canal was forced to close its gates in 1924, less than 100 years after its completion.

Today, however, it is one of the most successful and reliable resources in the nation. Its success comes not in profits, though, but

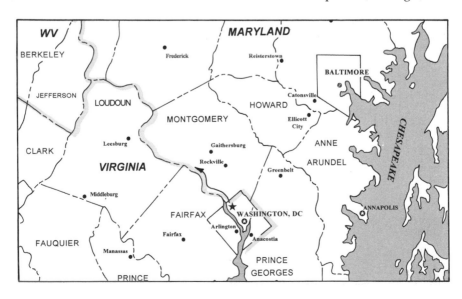

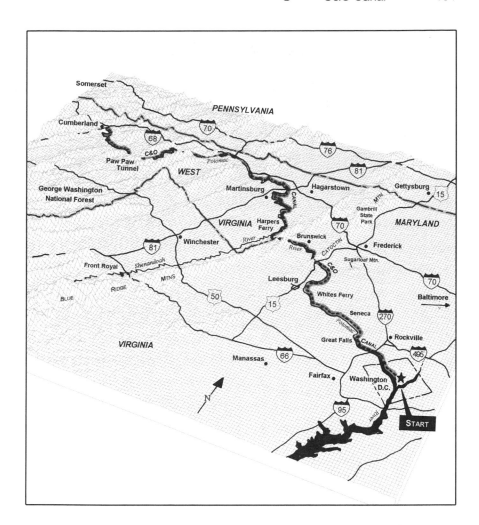

in the pleasure it provides to the thousands who hike, bike, or horseback along the crushed-stone-and natural-surfaced towpath each year. It is a reliable treasure chest of sights and wonders, delightful scenery, peace and solitude, and miles of serenity each day of the year. One of the best ways to enjoy the C&O Canal is to ride it in sections, beginning from different starting points. But there are plenty of camp sights along the towpath to accommodate a one-shot effort from Washington, D.C., to Cumberland.

The surface of the towpath is mostly dirt or crushed stone and remains in excellent condition. Due to floods, freezes, and tree roots, however, you should be prepared for some bumpy trails. Also, be aware that after heavy rainfall and times of high water, some sections

(continued on page 195)

C&O Canal

☞   **From the White House** – Take **Pennsylvania Avenue, NW,** toward **Georgetown**.   Go 11 blocks to **M Street**, turn **left** into **Georgetown**, and go two blocks to **Thomas Jefferson Street**. Turn **left** on **Thomas Jefferson Street**. **C&O Canal Visitors Center** here.

☞   **By Metro** – Take the Metro to **Foggy Bottom Metro station (Orange and Blue lines)**. Go **north** on **23rd Street** two blocks to **Washington Circle**. Go **counterclockwise** on Washington Circle to **Pennsylvania Avenue, NW**. Take **Pennsylvania Avenue, NW,** five blocks to **Georgetown**. From here, follow directions above.

MILES   DIRECTIONS

0.0   **START** at the **Georgetown Visitors Center** at the corner of Thomas Jefferson Street and M Street in Georgetown.

0.5   Fletcher's Boat House (bike rentals and repairs).

14.3   Great Falls Tavern Visitors Center.

22.8   Seneca Creek Aqueduct.

30.8   Edwards Ferry (not in operation).

35.5   Whites Ferry (last operating ferry on the Potomac).

42.2   Monocacy Aqueduct (largest aqueduct along the canal).

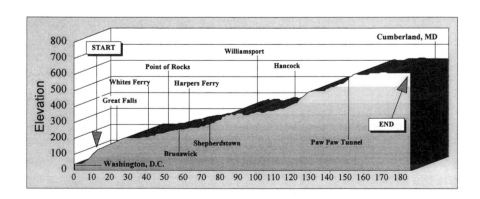

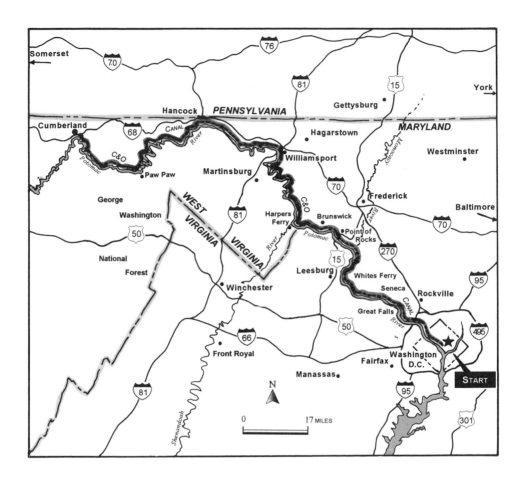

44.6   Nolands Ferry (not in operation).

48.2   Point of Rocks. Food available along Clay Street (Route 28).

55.0   Town of Brunswick. Telephone, food, and groceries.

60.8   Harpers Ferry. Telephone, food, and grocery store. Cross Appalachian Trail.

69.3   Antietam Creek Aqueduct. Ranger Station and camp.

72.7   Shepherdstown. Telephone, food, and groceries.

76.6   Sharpsburg. C&O Canal Park Headquarters.

99.8   Williamsport. Telephone, food, and groceries.

124.0   Hancock. Visitors Center. Telephone, food, and groceries.

156.0   Paw Paw Tunnel.

184.5   Reach Cumberland. C&O Canal towpath ends here. Telephone, food, groceries.

Ride Information

Trail Maintenance Hotline:

C&O Canal Headquarters   *(301) 739-4200*

Schedule:

Open from dawn til dusk every day of the year

Maps:

Delorme maps: Maryland road map; Virginia road map
ADC maps: Washington, D.C., road map
National Park Service C&O Canal trail map

(continued from page 191)

might be impassable. Just keep this in mind.

    With regard to the maps, don't be fooled by this ride's profile. It looks like an uphill battle all the way to Cumberland. Over 185 miles, however, a 600-foot elevation gain is virtually unnoticeable, and the trail will seem absolutely flat. Also, look closely at the 3D Map, and you can pick out the locations of some of the other rides in this book. Notice Sugarloaf Mountain, just below Frederick. Not so big anymore, is it?

C&O Canal towpath

Other Places to Ride

It's tough to map *all* the rides in this area and fit them into a single book. There really are so many. Those rides charted in this book are certainly some of the best in the Washington-Baltimore area, but absolutely not the only ones. Listed below are a few other great places to take the mountain bike and enjoy a day in the woods.

Frederick Watershed. Just north of Frederick, Maryland, adjacent to Gambrill State Park, Frederick Watershed is a fantastic mountain biking playground. There are miles of unpaved fire roads winding all over Catoctin Mountain, all of which are perfectly suitable for off-road bikes. The terrain is very steep and rugged, but if you're heading toward Gambrill or the Catoctin Blue Trail anyway, take a small detour and check out the Frederick Watershed.

Quantico Marine Base. There is some confusion about trail access in this huge wilderness just below Prince William Forest Park. The land is part of the Marine Corps Base, and many of the trails follow Marine training and obstacle courses. Some will say the trails (which happen to be great singletrack) are open to the public all the time, but you must first register with Range Control. Others (the higher in command on the base) say they have never allowed public access to the trails. Although mountain bike races are held on the Marine Base each year with little protest, call first before loading the bikes on the car.
Range Control — (703) 640-5321

Liberty Reservoir. North of Baltimore and just above the Mckeldin Area *(Ride #4)*, this reservoir contains many unpaved service roads great for mountain biking. However, mountain bike access is also uncertain here as well, so check with local bike shops or clubs before heading out there.

Ski Resorts
...for mountain biking?

Ski resorts offer a great alternative to local trail riding. During the spring, summer, and fall, many resorts will open their trails for mountain biking and, just like during ski season, sell lift tickets to take you and your bike to the top of the mountain. Lodging is also available for the weekend mountain bike junkies, and rates are often discounted from the normal ski-season prices. Some resorts will even rent bikes and lead guided mountain bike tours. Call ahead to find out just what each resort offers in the way of mountain bike riding, and pick the one that best suits your fancy.

Below is a list of all the ski resorts within 200 miles of the Washington-Baltimore area that say *yes!* to mountain biking when the weather turns too warm for skiing.

Whitetail	Mercersburg, PA	(717) 328-9400	89 miles
Liberty	Carrol Valley, PA	(717) 642-8282	90 miles
Bryce	Basye, VA	(703) 856-2121	97 miles
Massanutten	Harrisonburg, VA	(703) 289-9441	125 miles
Roundtop	Lewisberry, PA	(717) 432-9631	128 miles
Wintergreen	Waynesboro, VA	(804) 325-2200	150 miles
Blue Knob	Claysburg, PA	(814) 276-3576	165 miles
Timberline	Davis, WV	1-800-843-1751	185 miles
Canaan Valley	Davis, WV	(304) 866-4121	189 miles
Hidden Valley	Somerset, PA	(814) 443-2600	191 miles
Seven Springs	Somerset, PA	1-800-452-2223	195 miles
Wisp	McHenry, MD	(301) 387-4911	195 miles
Homestead	Hot Springs, VA	(703) 839-5500	200 miles
Snowshoe	Marlinton, WV	(304) 572-1000	210 miles

Appendix

Fletcher Harris

Repair and Maintain

FIXING A FLAT

Tools You Will Need

- Two tire irons
- Pump *(either a floor pump or a frame pump)*
- **No screwdrivers!!!** *(These can puncture the tube.)*

Removing the Wheel

The front wheel is easy. Simply open the quick release mechanism or undo the bolts with the proper sized wrench, then remove the wheel from the bike.

The rear wheel is a little more tricky. Before you loosen the wheel from the frame, shift the chain into the smallest gear on the freewheel *(the cluster of gears in the back)*. Once you've done this, removing and installing the wheel, like the front, is much easier.

Removing the Tire

STEP ONE — Insert a tire iron under the bead of the tire and pry the tire over the lip of the rim. Be careful not to pinch the tube when you do this.

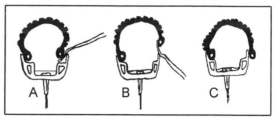

Pull the bead off the rim

STEP TWO — Hold the first tire iron in place. With the second tire iron, repeat *step one*, three or four inches down the rim. Alternate tire irons, pulling the bead of the tire over the rim, section by section, until one side of the tire bead is completely off the rim.

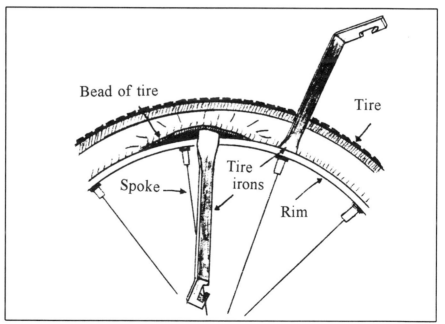

Using tire irons

STEP THREE — Remove the rest of the tire and tube from the rim. This can be done by hand. It's easiest to remove the valve stem last. Once the tire is off the rim, pull the tube out of the tire.

Clean and Safety Check

STEP FOUR — Using a rag, wipe the inside of the tire to clean out any dirt, sand, glass, thorns, etc. These may cause the tube to puncture. The inside of a tire should feel smooth. Any pricks or bumps could mean that you have found the culprit responsible for your flat tire.

STEP FIVE — Wipe the rim clean, then check the rim strip, making sure it covers the spoke nipples properly on the inside of the rim. If a spoke is poking through the rim strip, it could cause a puncture.

STEP SIX — At this point, you can do one of two things: replace the punctured tube with a new one, or patch the hole. It's easiest to just replace the tube with a new tube when you're out on the trails. Roll up the old tube and take it home to repair later that night in front of the TV. Directions on patching a tube are usually included with the patch kit itself.

Installing the Tire and Tube
(This can be done entirely by hand)

STEP SEVEN — Inflate the new or repaired tube with enough air to give it shape, then tuck it back into the tire.

STEP EIGHT — To put the tire and tube back on the rim, begin by putting the valve in the valve hole. The valve must be straight. Then use your hands to push the beaded edge of the tire onto the rim all the way around so that one side of your tire is on the rim.

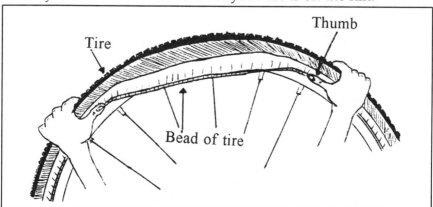

Wrestling a tire onto a rim

STEP NINE — Let most of the air out of the tube to allow room for the rest of the tire.

STEP TEN — Beginning opposite the valve, use your thumbs to push the other side of the tire onto the rim. Be careful not to pinch the tube in between the tire and the rim. The last few inches may be difficult, and you may need the tire iron to pry the tire onto the rim. If so, just be careful not to puncture the tube.

Before Inflating Completely

STEP ELEVEN — Check to make sure the tire is seated properly and that the tube is not caught between the tire and the rim. Do this by adding about 5 to 10 pounds of air, and watch closely that the tube does not bulge out of the tire.

STEP TWELVE — Once you're sure the tire and tube are properly seated, put the wheel back on the bike, then fill the tire with air. It's easier squeezing the wheel through the brake shoes if the tire is still flat.

STEP THIRTEEN — Now fill the tire with the proper amount of air, and check constantly to make sure the tube doesn't bulge from the rim. If the tube does appear to bulge out, release all the air as quickly as possible, or you could be in for a big bang.

When installing the rear wheel, place the chain back onto the smallest cog *(furthest gear on the right)*, and pull the derailleur out of the way. Your wheel should slide right on.

LUBRICATION AVOIDS DETERIORATION

Lubrication is crucial to maintaining your bike. Dry spots will be eliminated. Creaks, squeaks, grinding, and binding will be gone. The chain will run quietly, and the gears will shift smoothly. The brakes will grip quicker, and your bike may last longer with fewer repairs. Need I say more? Well, yes. Without knowing where to put the lubrication, what good is it?

Things You Will Need

- One can of bicycle lubricant, found at any bike store.
- A clean rag *(to wipe excess lubricant away).*

What Gets Lubricated

- Front derailleur
- Rear derailleur
- Shift levers
- Front brake
- Rear brake
- Both brake levers
- Chain

Where to Lubricate

To make it easy, simply spray a little lubricant on all the pivot points of your bike. If you're using a squeeze bottle, use just a drop or two. Put a few drops on each point wherever metal moves against metal, for instance, at the center of the brake calipers. Then let the lube sink in.

Once you have applied the lubricant to the derailleurs, shift the gears a few times, working the derailleurs back and forth. This allows the lubricant to work itself into the tiny cracks and spaces it must occupy to do its job. Work the brakes a few times as well.

Lubing the Chain

Lubricating the chain should be done after the chain has been wiped clean of most road grime. Do this by spinning the pedals counterclockwise while gripping the chain with a clean rag. As you add the lubricant, be sure to get some in between each link. With an aerosol spray, just spray the chain while pedaling backwards *(counterclockwise)* until the chain is fully lubricated. Let the lubricant soak in for a few seconds before wiping the excess away. Chains will collect dirt much faster if they're loaded with too much lubrication.

Frisbike!

Mountain Bike Clubs and Trail Groups

M.O.R.E. (Mid-Atlantic
Off Road Enthusiasts)
9504 Arlington Boulevard
Fairfax, VA 22031
(703) 631-2023
(703) 352-1660

Vertical Velo Club
10846 Grass Hill Park Rd
Frederick, MD 21702
(301) 846-1167
(301) 293-3691

Maryland Mountain Biking Club
10062 Carillon Drive
Ellicott City, MD 21042
(301) 314-0031

Urban Nomads
P.O. Box 3493
Alexandria, VA 22302-0493
(703) 379-8785

IMBA (International Mountain
Bicycling Association)
P.O.Box 412043
Los Angeles, CA 90041
(619) 387-2757

NORBA (National Off Road
Bicycle Association)
1750 East Boulder Street
Colorado Springs, CO 80909
(719) 578-4581

League of American Wheelmen
190 West Ostend Street #120
Baltimore, MD 21230-3731
(410) 539-3399

Rails-to-Trails Conservancy
1400 16th Street, NW, Suite 300
Washington, D.C. 20036-2222
(202) 797-5400

Other Area Bicycle Clubs

Regional

National Capital Velo Club
P.O. Box 14004
Washington, D.C. 20044--4004
(301) 779-1310
Racing oriented

Capital Cycle Challenge Club
14 Newbury Court
Gaithersburg, MD 20882-4005
(301) 253-5819

Potomac Pedalers Touring Club
P.O. Box 23601
Washington, D.C. 20026-3601
(202) 363-TOUR
Nation's largest local touring club

College Park Bicycle Club
4360 Knox Road
College Park, MD 20740-3171
(301) 779-4848
Racing oriented

W.A.B.A. (Washington Area
Bicycling Association)
1819 H Street NW, Suite 640
Washington, D.C. 20006-3603
(202) 872-9830

Frederick Pedalers Bicycle Club
P.O. Box 1293
Frederick, MD 21701-0293

Oxon Hill Bicycle Club
P.O. Box 81
Oxon Hill, MD 20750-0081
(301) 567-6760

Washington Women Outdoors
P.O. Box 301
Garrett Park, MD 20896-0301
(301) 864-3070
Offers day and overnight trips for women

Virginia

Arlington County Bicycle Club
300 North Park Drive
Arlington, VA 22203-2599
(703) 751-8929

Maryland

Baltimore Bicycle Club
P.O. Box 5906
Baltimore, MD 21208-0906
(410) 484-2740
Touring club

Reston Bicycle Club
P.O. Box 3389
Reston, VA 22090-1389
(703) 904-0900

Whole Wheel Velo Club
9514 Main Street
Fairfax, VA   22031-4031
(703) 323-0500
Racing Oriented

ABOUT THE AUTHOR

When not conquering fiery new trails on his mountain bike or racing from town to town on his road bike, Scott Adams is hard at work writing his next guidebook, trying to play guitar, or learning to cook with a wok. Scott, a long-time resident of the Washington area, is a free-lance writer and author who lives his life to be outdoors. Nothing, he says, is more therapeutic than a long hike to the top of a mountain or an early-morning bike ride with no particular place to go. His other books include *Bike Rides from Beaver Stadium: An Atlas of Centre County's Greatest Bicycle Rides* and *Mountain Bike Madness in Central PA: An Atlas of Central Pennsylvania's Greatest Mountain Bike Rides*.

Other books by Scott Adams

Mountain Bike Madness *in* Central PA
*An Atlas of Central Pennsylvania's Greatest
Mountain Bike Rides*

From the southern tip of Rothrock State Park
to the northern tier of Tiadaghton's Black Forest,
Mountain Bike Madness takes you over rugged singletrack, through abandoned tunnels, across narrow
train trestles, past magnificent vistas and along Central Pennsylvania's most scenic mountain roads and
trails. 18 rides highlighting the area's parks, natural
areas, and scenery make *Mountain Bike Madness* the
perfect guide to off-road adventures in Central
Pennsylvania's magnificent backcountry.

Soft cover, 144 pages, 6 x 9
$10.95   ISBN   1-882997-02-6

Bike Rides *from* Beaver Stadium
An Atlas of Centre County's Greatest Bicycle Rides

For **Nittany Lion** fans, each of the 24 rides in
this unique guidebook conveniently leaves from **Penn
State's Beaver Stadium!** Traveling in circuits of 5 miles
to over 100 miles long, each ride leads cyclists of all
ages and abilities along safe and comfortable roads,
highlighting Central Pennsylvania's scenic beauty,
historic landmarks, villages, towns, people, and food.
Its unique, hand-drawn maps, complete with barking
dogs, stop signs, and cows, give this book a real sense
of intimacy with the roads and the region. *Bike Rides
from Beaver Stadium* is the perfect guide to bicycling in
Centre County, Pennsylvania.

Soft cover, 128 pages, 6 x 9
$9.95   ISBN   1-882997-01-8

Ask for these books at your local bookstore or outdoor store
— or —
order them directly from

Beachway Press
9201 Beachway Lane
Springfield, VA 22153